I0454790

●●●●●●●●●●●●●●●●●●●●●●●●●●●●

IMPACT 2.0 – NEW MECHANISMS FOR LINKING RESEARCH AND POLICY

Editors:
Bruce Girard
Estela Acosta y Lara

● ●

Impact 2.0 – New Mechanisms for Linking Research and Policy

Editors: Bruce Girard and Estela Acosta y Lara

Published in 2012 by Fundación Comunica – Pablo de María 1036 – Montevideo, Uruguay <www.comunica.org>

Graphic design: Rodolfo Fuentes/NAO

ISBN 978-1479 1314 5 7

IMPACT 2.0 – NEW MECHANISMS FOR LINKING RESEARCH AND POLICY

The research presented in this report was conducted during 2010 – 2011, funded by the International Development Research Centre (IDRC, Canada) and coordinated by Fundación Comunica with support from the Association for Progressive Communications (APC).

● ●

CONTENTS

New mechanisms for linking research and policy
What is Impact 2.0?

Impact 2.0: New mechanisms for linking research and policy supported a series of small[1] research projects examining the use of online social networking services to link research and policy in Latin America. Twelve projects were supported, most of them selected from ninety-seven proposals received following the distribution of a call for proposals in May 2010. Two types of projects were supported: (i) action research projects involved both implementing and evaluating a specific use of one or more online social networking services to link research and policy or researchers and policymakers, and (ii) more conventional ones evaluated existing initiatives implemented by third parties.

A five-member jury[2] evaluated the submissions and its members provided advice and support to the researchers at various moments during the project, but no specific framework

---

1 Budgets ranged from $6,000 to a maximum of $20,000.

2 The members of the jury were Valeria Betancourt (APC), Clio Bugel and Bruce Girard (Fundación Comunica), Ana Laura Rivoir (Universidad de la República, Uruguay) and César Herrera (CIESPAL).

1

or theoretical approach was imposed. Proposals were accepted from a variety of disciplinary perspectives as long as they addressed, through a formal research process, the impact of web 2.0 and online social networking services on the links between research and public policy, with an overall objective of documenting the design, implementation and impact of actions undertaken to link of knowledge generation and policy definition.

Four assumptions underlined Impact 2.0's call for proposals:

1. That public policy processes are complex and involve a variety of stakeholders, interests, constraints and opportunities;

2. That research can make a valuable contribution to better public policy;

3. That communication plays a key role in the relationship between research and policy –including how research findings are communicated (e.g. academic reports or policy briefs), who they are communicated to (e.g. directly to policymakers, to other stakeholders and to thematic networks, or to the media and the public at large) and how relationships between the various actors and stakeholders are managed;

4. That the expanding role of the internet is changing the way that researchers and policymakers communicate and, more specifically, that online social networking services offer fertile ground for experimentation and evaluation of initiatives.

POLICY, RESEARCH COMMUNICATION AND THE INTERNET

Policy development is a complex process and there are many reasons why even the best proposals backed by solid research can fail to be heard or to be acted on. Decision makers are barraged with conflicting demands, often supported by contradictory evidence, making it difficult for independent research to even be considered. Lack of transparency and political will, bureaucratic inertia, low levels of public understanding of and interest in policy issues, and counter arguments promoted by interests with their own agendas in mind further complicate the scenario. Other complications arise when researchers and policymakers do not share a common agenda –resulting in carefully researched solutions to problems that policymakers are not trying to address.

Even when the importance of independent public-interest research in supporting policy development is widely-accepted, when the research is solid and designed to help resolve the recognised problems of policymakers, advocacy groups and other stakeholders, and when policy-making institutions are transparent and adequately resourced, research faces significant challenges to being effectively introduced into policy debates.

In her book *Saber y Política en América Latina* (2007) Mercedes Botto identifies two paradigms that attempt to explain how research results influence policy-making in Latin America. The first of these sees a rationalist and linear approach in which researchers have the clearly-defined task of producing knowledge and proposing solutions based on empirical evidence and policymakers are charged with implementing these solutions. In this paradigm, if the data is available, the analysis rigorous, the timing right, and the conclusions clear and not in conflict with other political interests, then the right policies will emerge. However, this attractively simple view of the relationship failed to explain why, as Weiss wryly observed, "neglecting research findings was a common recreation in arenas of action" (2009).

Botto's second paradigm is more complex and recognizes the important roles played by other actors and external factors, and "that there is not 'one' but 'multiple' decision-making arenas that are juxtaposed and self-regulated through a process of mutual adjustment. Various actors, with partial information and diverse knowlege, participate in this decision-making process".

Seen in the light of this paradigm, policy research is one of many inputs and its impact depends on how well its conclusions and proposals compete with or conform to others, how it is inserted into multiple forums, and how it reaches multiple actors. In this more realistic view of the relationship between research and policy the role of communication is both crucial and complex. It is still important to communicate with policymakers, but it is not enough. Researchers must also engage with counter-proposals, get their messages across to multiple actors (including potential allies, adversaries and at times even the general public), and manage communication activities across multiple arenas and within overlapping networks.

Recent initiatives seeking to better understand and to strengthen the relationship between research and policy have also emphasised the key role played by communication. The Overseas Development Institute's (ODI) *Research and Policy in Development Programme* (RAPID), for example, lists communication as one of its core research and training interests, the others being the role of evidence in the policy process, institutional development and knowledge management[3] Likewise, the IDRC-led *Think Tank Initiative*[4], provides support in three areas: (i) communication, (ii) research methods and skills and (iii) general organizational development.

A number of factors are behind this new emphasis on communication, including: (i) the recognition that development research is of limited value if it stays on the shelves, (ii) the need to demonstrate research impact, (iii) a quest for more evidence based policy & practice, (iv) more competition among research players and, (v) key to the studies presented in this report, the many changes that are accompanying the expanding role of the internet in research, research communication and policy formulation. (Barnard et al: 2007)

---

3 www.odi.org.uk/RAPID/

4 www.idrc.ca/EN/Programs/Social_and_Economic_Policy/Think_Tank_Initiative

The internet is indeed changing the way that researchers and policymakers communicate. In 2000 a World Bank study evaluated the use of the internet by developing country policymakers and found that it was rated as the least important source of information.[5] Twelve years later, it is hard to imagine a policymaker who does not value the internet as an essential resource. Advances in ICTs and their use by governments, researchers, civil society and the media are clearly changing the rules governing the relationship between research and policy. For example:

- developments in e-governance and e-participation can enable increased transparency and accountability of policymakers and processes, and facilitate more fluid communication between policymakers, researchers and civil society organisations;
- the myriad of emerging social networking tools and applications offer new ways of building and coordinating networks, alliances and forums and of managing relationships with stakeholders;[6]
- online campaigning is emerging as a powerful advocacy tool;
- traditional print and broadcast media are making increasing use of interactive internet applications, opening up possible new avenues of communicating research and policy proposals and enabling wider discussion.

The studies included in this report are particularly focused on online social networking understood as "activities, practices and behaviors among communities of people who gather online to share information, knowledge and opinions using

5 MacDonald, Lawrence. (2000) 'Research Dissemination and Electronic Communication', Washington D.C., DECVP, World Bank.

6 There is even a specialised global network for scientists and researchers. ResearchGate, "the professional network for scientists and researchers", brings 1.7 million researchers together in a Facebook-like online environment.

conversational media... Web-based applications that make it possible to create and easily transmit content in the form of words, pictures, videos and audios."[7]

CONTEXT, EVIDENCE AND LINKS

As noted earlier, the individual research projects included under the Impact 2.0 umbrella were multi-disciplinary and no specific theoretical framework was imposed. Nevertheless the four assumptions mentioned earlier in this article were embedded in the call for proposals and the overall research proposal was guided by the context, evidence, links framework developed by the Overseas Development Institute's *Research and Policy in Development* (RAPID) programme to help think tanks and other research organisations influence development policy.[8] Rather than view the link between research and policy as a linear process whereby research findings simply shift (or don't) to the policy sphere, the framework encourages the analysis of the political context (institutions, power relations and other contextual factors that affect how policy is made), evidence produced by academic research, and the key links that can be made with organisations, networks and intermediaries with interest in the sector (policymakers, advocacy groups, the media).

In this framework the political context is a dimension concerned with how decisions are made and by whom. In some cases these are relatively easy to understand, managed by strong institutions and characterised by transparancy. In others things are more opaque and it is difficult to identify who is making decisions and what evidence or interests policies are based on. Formal institutions are one part of the context, but so are the interests

7 Lon Safko and David Brake, "The Social Media Bible - The Business Executive's Guide to Social Media", 2009. p. 7.

8 See the ODI paper Bridging Research and Policy in International Development for more information at www.odi.org.uk/RAPID/Publications/Documents/rapid_bp1_web.pdf (accessed 04/11/11)

and influence of other stakeholders, electoral considerations, corruption, and a multitude of other factors.

Evidence refers to the knowledge produced by academic research whether it be conducted by universities, think tanks, government departments, NGOs or consultant firms. It includes the evidence that researchers seek, evidence they have, evidence that current policy is based on and evidence supporting counter-arguments. This dimension is also concerned with the credibility and legitimacy of the organisations conducting the research, the form in which the research is presented and whether it actually provides solutions to the problems being considered.

Finally, given that government policy affects multiple interests within a society, many different groups could be interested in influencing decision making processes, for equally different motives and through multiple actions. To understand who these actors, to develop relationships with them and to build networks and alliances with those working toward common goals are activities that fall within the links dimension.

Table 1 shows how the framework can be applied by moving from a series of relatively simple questions in the first column, to identifying objectives and finally the tactics for achieving them.

The research projects were encouraged to consider this framework and to experiment with or analyse the use of the internet in general and online social networking services in particular at various stages of the exercise. For example, the institutional website of a ministry is a good place to start when looking for information about the policy context such as who the authorities are and their current priorities, but it is increasingly common for ministers and top civil servants to use services such as Twitter and Facebook. Information gleaned from these sources may be updated more frequently and its less formal nature can help complete the institutional profile on the official website.

Table 1 – Context, Evidence, Links – How to influence policy and practice

	What researchers need to know?	What researchers need to do?	How to do it?
Political Context	• Who are the policymakers? • Is there policymaker demand for new ideas? • What are the sources / strengths of resistance? • What is the policymaking process? • What are the opportunities and timing for input into formal processes?	• Get to know the policymakers, their agendas and their constraints. • Identify potential supporters and opponents. • Keep an eye on the horizon and prepare for opportunities in regular policy processes. • Look out for –and react to– unexpected policy windows.	• Work with the policymakers. • Seek commissions. • Line up research programmes with high-profile public policy events. • Reserve resources to be able to move quickly to respond to policy windows.
Evidence	• What is the current theory? • What are the prevailing narratives? • How divergent is the new evidence? • What sort of evidence will convince policymakers?	• Establish credibility over the long term. • Provide practical solutions to problems. • Establish legitimacy. • Build a convincing case and present clear policy options. • Package new ideas in familiar theory or narratives.	• Build up programmes of high-quality work. • Action-research and Pilot projects to demonstrate benefits of new approaches. • Participatory approaches help with legitimacy and implementation. • Clear strategy for communication. • Face-to-face communication.
Links	• Who are the key stakeholders? • What links and networks exist between them? • Who are the intermediaries, and do they have influence? • Whose side are they on?	• Get to know the other stakeholders. • Establish a presence in existing networks. • Build coalitions with like-minded stakeholders. • Build new policy networks.	• Partnerships between researchers, policymakers and policy end-users. • Identify key networkers and salesmen. • Use informal contacts.

Source: *Bridging Research and Policy in International Development*, ODI, 2004.

Key to the success of the context, evidence, links framework is the establishment of ongoing relationships between key stakeholders such as policymakers, researchers, civil society advocacy groups and private sector players. These relationships, both formal and informal, facilitate the insertion of research results into the policy process and enable researchers to verify the relevance and timeliness of their research agendas and to fully participate in ongoing policy discussions. A few of the research projects presented in this report sought to involve stakeholders in online collaboration around specific outputs as part of a strategy to encourage and support multi-sectoral relationships. Both Claeh's efforts to use a wiki to involve policymakers, academics, and NGOs to draft definitions of key concepts for social development policy and EVIPNet's use of a social networking platform to support the collective drafting of policy briefs were designed to producing concrete outputs and to create an online space where the various actors could work together and develop trust.[9]

Online social networking services might also be useful sources of information about real world links and networks, for identifying potential allies and for building coalitions and campaigns. The Impact 2.0 iGuide[10], which was prepared and published as a wiki during the early phase of the research, contains dozens of ideas for how to use social networking and web 2.0.

While some projects did use social networking services for actions in the first two columns, most of the attention was on the tactical dimension of influencing activities with a focus on three ways of influencing policy: (i) evidence and advice, (ii) public campaigns and advocacy and (iii) lobbying and negotiation (Jones, 2011). Table 2 shows channels and activities typically associated with influencing policy.

---

9 See chapter 7 in this report.

10 See the presentation of the iGuide in chapter 8 of this report and consult the iGuide online at iguides.comunica.org/ in English and iguias.comunica.org/ in Spanish.

Table 2: Typology of influencing activities

Type of influencing	Where? Through what channels?	How? By what means?
Evidence and advice	• National and international policy discourses/debates. • Formal and informal meetings.	• Reserch and analysis, "good practice". • Evidence-based argument. • Providing advisory support. • Developing and piloting new policy approaches.
Public campaigns and advocacy	• Public and political debates in developing countries. • Public meetings, speeches, presentations. • Television, newpapers, radio and other media.	• Public communications and campaings. • "Public education". • Messaging. • Advocacy.
Lobbying and negotiation	• Formal meetings. • Semi-formal and informal channels. • Membership and participation in boards and committees.	• Face-to-face meetings and discussions. • Relationships and trust. • Direct incentives and diplomacy.

Source: Jones (2011)

Once again Impact 2.0 projects were encouraged to experiment with and analyse the use of the internet and online social networking services in policy influencing activities. Some of the cases studied, that of Chile's Educación 2020 for example, successfully combined online and offline strategies in all of these areas in such a way that their online public campaigns helped prise open the doors to private meetings with policymakers, gave added weight to their presence in formal meetings, and focused attention on formal research outputs.

CAMPAIGNS, CONSULTATIONS AND DIRECT COMMUNICATION

While the experiments and evaluations undertaken under the Impact 2.0 umbrella displayed a tremendous diversity in terms of the online tools they used, their methodological approaches, their communication strategies etc., certain patterns emerged and overall the various projects can be seen to have adopted three distinct approaches to their use of social networking to link research and policy:

1. Projects in which researchers made use of online campaigns to make their research conclusions more visible to the public at large, usually with the expectation that public support and visibility would give their proposals increased legitimacy and support among policymakers.

2. Projects in which researchers sought to support online public consultation processes in collaboration with government entities.

3. Projects which explored the use of web 2.0 and social networking services to open direct channels of communication between researchers, policymakers and other stakeholders in order to communicate research, collaborate on specific activities, and/or with a more-or-less explicit objective of getting them to know each other better and to build trust.

For the Impact 2.0 projects the most successful uses of web 2.0 and online social networking to connect research and policy were those that involved the public in campaigns and consultations. Less successful were those projects that focused on the direct relationships between researchers, policymakers and other stakeholders

This report is divided into three main sections: (I) *Researcher-led campaigns*, (II) *Online public consultations* and (III) *Explorations*.

Researcher-led campaigns

Social media campaigns abound in the 21st century. Politicians dedicate significant resources to online campaigns, which in turn can generate significant revenue[11] while advertisers and activists alike hope their videos go "viral", with links and comments about them spreading rapidly through social networks, eventually being exposed to tens of millions of people. Some people even go so far as to credit social media campaigns with overthrowing governments, for example during 2011's so-called "Arab Spring" uprisings in Tunisia and Egypt.[12]

Researchers and think tanks are also experimenting with social media campaigns, albeit less massively and dramatically than the examples above, in efforts to ensure that their research conclusions become part of public discussions of policy options.

The section looks at two cases of researcher-led campaigns to influence public policy in Latin America: *Educación 2020*, a campaign to introduce certain reforms in Chile's public education system, and the work of the *Impact 2.0 National laboratory for Peru* that used a variety of online tools and strategies to effectively introduce research results to the national broadband policy debate.

Educación 2020

The first case, *Internet, Research and Influence: The strategies of Educación 2020*, tells the story of a campaign initiated by an influential academic and a small group of students that

11 Barack Obama's 21 month campaign for the 2008 US presidential elections raised more than US$500,000,000 online. voices.washingtonpost.com/44/2008/11/obama-raised-half-a-billion-on.html(last accessed 23/04/2012)

12 Others are more skeptical. Evgeny Morozov, for example, argues that crediting Facebook and Twitter with the Arab Spring is more a product of the West's "starry-eyed digital fervor" than of Arab "cyberactivism" (2011)

harnessed the power of web 2.0 to amplify their voices, generate a movement with tens of thousands of supporters, and open the doors to the highest level of policy making. The authors paint a picture of Educación 2020 as a sort of hybrid organisation that combined online and offline strategies of think tanks, social movements, foundations and lobbyists to achieve a high level of impact in multiple arenas, including the media, public forums, online platforms, and in private meetings with top-level policymakers, including cabinet ministers and the president.

There is no single key to Educación 2020's success but some of the factors that contributed to it include:

- It was able to leverage the considerable political capital of its founder, leader and primary spokesperson, an academic who had established credentials and contacts;
- Its online messages were simple and Educación 2020 clearly articulated how concerned citizens could support the initiative;
- Its demands were adapted to the political context and formulated in a way that made them attractive to policymakers and the public;
- The social networking campaign was not the end in itself but it contributed to an overall strategy that combined more traditional lobbying. Educación 2020 would never have been able to gather its 80,000 online supporters for a mass demonstration, but it was able to use them to support its efforts to have the press and the public perceive it as a legitimate social movement worthy of debating the powerful teachers union and the students' movement.

As the authors of the study conclude, "extensive use of internet to generate public support is not enough to enable social movements [or think tanks] to effectively participate in public policy discussion in Chile. On the contrary... the capacity to formulate proposals making clear technical contributions to on-going discussion, and the existence of political networks, are all still key factors for success." Nevertheless, ICTs do "open up possibilities by which organisations, think tanks and research centres with technically sound policy agendas can seek public support via the internet, achieving a certain citizen-endowed legitimacy for their proposals."

A national laboratory 2.0 in Peru

The second case looked at is that of the Impact 2.0 national laboratory in Peru. Set up as part of the Impact 2.0 project the laboratory was provided with minimal resources and given a broad mandate to experiment with using online social networking tools to link ICT research and policy. Unlike the Educación 2020 chapter, which is the result of an external review of the initiative, the Peruvian chapter was written by the project leader and describes the experience from the inside.

Following an analysis of the policy context, the laboratory selected a theme and existing research that could contribute to the discussion, identified the main stakeholders, and developed a communication strategy that combined online social networking services with more traditional tools such as policy briefs and seminars.

The strategy adopted included three phases: (i) generate interest in the theme by demonstrating its importance; (ii) contribute to understanding of the issues and options with a policy brief and meetings with stakeholders, and (iii) create online and offline opportunities for participation.

Among the conclusions of the case study is that while tools like Twitter and Facebook work when the message is precise and of general interest and the goal is to register support (as in the case of Educación 2020), they are not so useful when the goal is to bring stakeholders together for more substantial discussion and exchange of knowledge about more complex issues. Face-to-face meetings are generally seen as better for this but an experiment with internet TV succeeded in attracting the attention and participation of key actors, including some of those not normally inclined to participate in open public debates. Whether internet TV is a new possibility, or its success was due to its novelty attraction, remains an open question.

Online public consultations

One way governments can improve their policy proposals is by submitting them to the test of public opinion. Public consultations involve soliciting public and stakeholder input into the policymaking process. Through consultations, policymakers can involve expertise and alternative perspectives in the discussion, or identify opposing interests and invite ideas for how they might be balanced. Consultations can be formal or informal, they can be limited to a handful of key stakeholders, or invite comments from the general public, and they can take place in a single moment or as part of ongoing deliberation. Whatever form they take, the key objectives include to improve the quality of information available to decision-makers, to give citizens and stakeholders a role in discussing policy options and, ultimately, to contribute to better policy.

Traditional consultation processes are conducted during meetings or by inviting the submission of briefs or opinions. Meetings have the advantage of permitting dialogue between and among stakeholders and government, while on the downside they impose severe physical and time constraints – face-to-face dialogue requires everyone to be at the same place at the same time. Inviting written interventions, on the other hand, overcomes problems of time and space, but inhibits dialogue.

The section looks at how the interactive possibilities of the internet were employed to support public consultation processes, convened by policymakers and researchers, that overcome the problems of space and time inherent in consultations based on meetings and written interventions, focusing on recent *consultation 2.0* experiences in Brazil and Uruguay. The authors evaluate the role of institutions and political practitioners in designing such initiatives in two case studies: a Brazilian initiative to draft legislation on internet governance (the Marco Civil Regulatorio or MCR), and an Uruguayan public consultation on digital television broadcasting. In their analysis the authors seek to:

1. formulate hypotheses on what contextual elements favour the launch of online consultations;
2. evaluate how deliberative rules and technology overlap; and
3. map good practices regarding the mix of different web 2.0 technologies for designing online deliberation experiences for drafting legislation and policy.

While the case studies point to the value of involving various stakeholders in public consultations, the evidence indicates that governmental commitment is essential. The Brazilian initiative was led by the Ministry of Justice with the active involvement of the Ministry of Culture and the *Centro de Tecnologia e Sociedade*, a civil society think tank. While the participation of the think tank brought a number of advantages, the consultation was convened and led by the government and the result –draft legislation for governing the internet– was an official document.

This contrasts with Uruguay where the Ministry of Industry, Energy and Mining (MIEM) proposed the virtual public hearing, but then progressively withdrew its support, first declining to convene it, then organising a formal but parallel *public notice-and-comment process*, and finally excluding the results of the consultation from the formal process.

The report compares the differences and similarities of the two consultations, identifies some lessons learned, and points to areas requiring further research. The authors suggest that, despite the pioneering nature of the projects and their very different contexts, both experiences had to deal with similar challenges in mixing policy making, technology and society. Among the key lessons learned are:

1. Online public consultations require openness. Governments and bureaucracies must be open to consulting with citizens on topics of general public interest or public consultations, online or otherwise, will not be successful. For online consultations they must also be willing to use unfamiliar tools and, more importantly, be willing to engage in unfamiliar practices whose very strength lies in their transparency and accessibility. These challenges can require changes in the institutional cultures of governmental institutions more comfortable with announcing decisions than asking for advice.

2. Government institutions matter, a lot. In addition to being open to the idea, successful online consultations require the active support of the sponsoring government institution. Stakeholders and citizens will only engage with the process if they believe the sponsoring institution is taking it seriously and they will be listened to.

3. Researchers and think tanks can play various roles in online consultations. In the cases studied these included designing the consultations, deciding what technologies to incorporate, moderating, providing context and presenting issues and options, and facilitating contact with civil society initiatives.

4. As with any policy consultation, the topic being discussed matters. If people perceive their interests are at stake, they will be more likely to participate. However, online consultations may have their own bias built-in and part of the success of Brazil's consultation can be partially explained by the fact that its topic, internet governance, was perceived as important by "cyberactivists", a community particularly qualified and accustomed to online deliberation.

Explorations

While campaigns and public consultations were the areas where our research had the most complete results, the many small projects conducted under the Impact 2.0 umbrella also analysed other areas, prepared materials to support further experimentation, learned lessons and in some cases simply stumbled upon unexpected emerging trends and uses of online social networking services for linking research and policy.

For example, some projects attempted to bring researchers, policymakers and other stakeholders together in online spaces with the more-or-less explicit objective of getting them to know each other better and to build trust. Others examined whether various stakeholders are ready to use the new tools and applications and attempted to identify the barriers to their use in terms of access, capacity, interest, and policy. Another of the project's outputs was the *Impact 2.0 iGuide*, a wiki-based manual designed to help researchers use social networking tools (i) to better understand the policy context; (ii) to encourage discussion, debate and collaboration based on their research findings; and (iii) to develop and maintain relations with policy makers and other stakeholders.

The Explorations section of this report brings together these preliminary experiences as short case studies, research reports, and articles that identify areas for future research.

It also includes a short article about the Impact 2.0 *iGuide* and a report of a research project coordinated by the Centro Internacional de Estudios Superiores en Comunicación para América Latina-CIESPAL- about the use of social networks by the public service in five countries of the region.

***

The 2001 OECD report, 'Citizens as Partners' noted that citizen engagement with policy making has three dimensions:

information, consultation and active participation.[13] A subsequent OECD report on e-democracy looked at how online engagement could "ensure greater accessibility of more information" and how to harness "the interactivity of ICTs for online consultation".[14] In general terms, the cases looked at in the Impact 2.0 project have demonstrated that the incorporation of web 2.0 and social networking services have opened up new and powerful opportunities for e-engagement beyond information provision and consultation in the direction of active participation and collaboration between stakeholders.

The research presented here demonstrates that web 2.0 and online social networking services can be productively employed in researcher-led campaigns and online public consultations that seek to increase the impact of research on public policy and that the tools can also be used to support collaboration between researchers and other stakeholders.

It is also evident that prior to their use certain conditions must be in place and that they are best employed as part of a multi-faceted communication strategy. If policymakers are not able or willing to use the tools, if they are not interested in changing the policy, or if they are not open to the evidence being presented or to its source, then web 2.0 tools are unlikely to increase research impact. On the other hand, if the contextual conditions are met, researchers with solid and relevant proposals can effectively and economically incorporate web 2.0 and online social networking into an overall communication strategy.

While any conclusions stemming from the research reported in this publication are necessarily tentative, interactive internet applications and services have undeniably had an impact across multiple domains – altering personal and professional relations, enabling collaboration across time and space, reducing

13 OECD: Citizens as Partners: OECD Handbook on Information, Consultation and Public Participation in Policy Making, 2001

14 OECD: Promise and Problems of E-Democracy: Challenges of Online Citizen Engagement, 2003

communication costs, facilitating network development and permitting new ways of creating, sharing, discussing and accessing knowledge. The research conducted under the Impact 2.0 umbrella shows that the tools have the potential to contribute to better linkages between research and policy and begins to explore the conditions, uses and strategies that will enable that potential.

CAMPAIGNS LED
BY RESEARCHERS

1. INTRODUCTION

Bruce Girard

Social media campaigns abound in the 21st century. Politicians dedicate significant resources to online campaigns, which in turn can generate significant revenue[1] while advertisers and activists alike hope their videos go "viral", with links and comments about them spreading rapidly through social networks, eventually being exposed to tens of millions of people. Some people even go so far as to credit social media campaigns with overthrowing governments, for example during 2011's so-called "Arab Spring" uprisings in Tunisia and Egypt.

Researchers and think tanks are also experimenting with social media campaigns, albeit less massively and dramatically than the examples mentioned above, in efforts to ensure that their research conclusions become part of public discussions of policy options.

---

1 Barack Obama's 21 month campaign for the 2008 US presidential elections raised more than US$500,000 online. voices.washingtonpost.com/44/2008/11/obama-raised-half-a-billion-on.html (last accessed 23/04/2012)

In this section we look at two cases of researcher-led campaigns to influence public policy in Latin America: *Educación 2020* (E2020), a campaign to introduce certain reforms in Chile's public education system and the work of Impact 2.0's national laboratory in Peru on broadband policy.

EDUCACIÓN 2020

The first case, *Internet, Research and Influence: The Strategies of Educación 2020*, tells the story of a group founded by an influential academic and a small group of students that harnessed the power of web 2.0 to amplify their voices, generate a movement with tens of thousands of supporters, and open the doors to the highest level of policy making. The authors paint a picture of E2020 as a sort of hybrid organisation that combined online and offline strategies of think tanks, social movements, foundations and lobbyists to achieve a high level of impact in multiple arenas, including the media, public forums, online platforms, and in private meetings with top-level policymakers, including cabinet ministers and the president.

There is no single key to E2020's success but some of the factors that contributed to it include:

- From the very beginning it was able to leverage the considerable political capital of its founder, leader and primary spokesperson, an academic who had established credentials and contacts. Whether an individual or a think tank, it helps to have recognised expertise behind you before starting a campaign;

- Its online messages were simple and E2020 clearly articulated how concerned citizens could support the initiative;

- Its demands were adapted to the political context and formulated in a way that made them attractive to policymakers and the public. No matter how much they were supported by evidence, E2020 would not have been granted an audience with the president on the basis of *virtual* support for its demands if they went against the government's own interests;

- The social networking campaign was not the end in itself but it contributed to an overall strategy that combined more traditional lobbying. E2020 would never have been able to gather its 80,000 online supporters for a mass demonstration, but it was able to use them to support its efforts to have the press and the public perceive it as a legitimate social movement worthy of debating the teachers union and the students'movement.

As the authors of the study conclude, "extensive use of internet to generate public support is not enough to enable social movements [or think tanks] to effectively participate in public policy discussion in Chile. On the contrary... the capacity to formulate proposals making clear technical contributions to on-going discussion, and the existence of political networks, are all still key factors for success." Nevertheless, ICTs do "open up possibilities by which organisations, think tanks and research centres with technically sound policy agendas can seek public support via the internet, achieving a certain citizen-endowed legitimacy for their proposals."

A NATIONAL LABORATORY 2.0 IN PERU

The second case looked at is that of the Impact 2.0 national laboratory in Peru. Set up as part of the Impact 2.0 project the laboratory was provided with minimal resources and given a broad mandate to experiment with using web 2.0 tools to link ICT research and policy. The project leader, Jorge Bossio, was coordinator of the Latin American research network DIRSI (Regional Dialogue on the Information Society), a former employee of Peru's telecommunication regulator, and a member of various academic and civil society networks and thus well-placed to serve a role linking various ICT policy initiatives. Unlike the E2020 chapter, which is the result of an external review of the initiative, the Peruvian chapter was written by the project leader and describes the experience from the inside.

The Peruvian laboratory first analysed the policy context, selected a theme, selected existing research that could contribute to the discussion, identified the main stakeholders, and developed a communication strategy that combined web 2.0 with more traditional tools such as policy briefs and seminars.

The strategy adopted included three phases: (i) generate interest in the theme by demonstrating its importance; (ii) contribute to understanding of the issues and options with a policy brief and meetings with stakeholders, and (iii) create online and offline opportunities for participation – of particular interest to this final phase was *Código Abierto*, an internet-only television programme created by the laboratory in cooperation with *La Mula*, one of Peru's most important news portals. *Código Abierto* produced five programmes with guests that included policymakers, representatives of the private sector, academia and civil society. The experience with Facebook for linking key actors was less successful. The Facebook pages set up to facilitate discussion around the issues were used by civil society organisations and eventually caught the interest of the government's advisory commission on broadband policy, which invited the laboratory to present the results of the debate to a meeting of the commission. However, while commission members were aware of the debate in Facebook, they were unable to participate in it or even to see the content –access to Facebook is blocked from government offices in Peru.

Among the conclusions of the case study is that while tools like Twitter and Facebook work when the message is precise and of general interest and the goal is to register support (as in the case of Educación 2020), they are not so useful when the goal is to bring stakeholders together for more substantial discussion and exchange of knowlege about more complex issues (possible models for implementation and regulation of the national internet backbone). Face-to-face meetings are generally seen as better for this but the experiment with internet TV succeeded in attracting the attention and participation of key actors, including some of those not normally inclined to participate in open public debates. Whether internet TV is a new possibility, or *Código Abierto's* success is due to its novelty attraction, is an open question.

2. INTERNET, RESEARCH AND INFLUENCE: THE STRATEGIES OF EDUCACIÓN 2020

Eduardo Araya and Diego Barría

INTRODUCTION

The internet is a key means of communication in the daily lives of people and politics in Chile. Although only 40% of households reported having an internet connection at home in 2009, 53% of the population said they were internet users (SUBTEL 2010).

One of the most interesting aspects of the internet in Chile is that evidence is appearing that it has become a virtual space where state and politics are present. The number of citizens who connect to the internet for government transactions is high (Araya and Barría 2008); also, new communities are being organized through the net, centred on public policy topics and even for presenting alternative presidential candidates (Araya, Barría and Campos, 2009). The internet is thus not outside the scope of political discussion; on the contrary, it has become fertile ground for the organization of collective action, especially for those seeking to influence socially relevant issues (Castells 1997).

Our research is concerned with this last statement, and seeks to find whether internet use allows Chilean society to link visible social movements to influence public debate in general, and policy formulation in particular, and, if it does, to see how it has been used.

It is worth noting that new kinds of social organizations were found in Chile by the end of the 1970s, organised around citizens' interests but controlled by think tanks or research centres run by people with technical profiles. These think tanks sought to influence public policies (Silva 2008), in a context in which citizen participation was reduced to discussions based on technical details (Márquez 2010).

Our research specifically assesses *Educación 2020* (E2020), an initiative of this type created in 2008 by Mario Waissbluth, a distinguished Chilean academic with a career at the Universidad de Chile and experience as a board member for various public institutions and university organisations in his capacity as expert in public administration. E2020's aim is to promote a national debate on educational policies with the goal of ensuring that the poorest 20% of Chile's children have the same education opportunities as the richest 20% by the year 2020.

We selected E2020 for this study because it was initially created and organized almost exclusively via internet, achieving rapid visibility through the debate on educational policies, to the point that it was recognized by government authorities and parliament as an actor within the sector and, after only two years, 80,000 people had signed on as supporters of its proposals. In addition to a think tank, E2020 appears to be a successful internet-based social organization with the goal of influencing public policies.

Our research did not seek to measure E2020's degree of success in its attempt to influence Chilean educational policies. However, our starting point was the fact that the movement's success was demonstrated by its being recognised by the government as a relevant actor with which to discuss education policy. Taking this as our starting point, we hoped to discover whether the internet was responsible for E2020 securing this privileged position, or whether it was due to more traditional factors.

We concentrated on E2020's internet strategy over 2008 to 2011, on its participation in the institutional education policy discussion forums of the Ministry of Education, and parliamentary committees), and on the factors that enabled its participation in these forums.

The study was based on field-work, which took the form of interviews with key sources, including E2020 members, Ministry of Education officials and members of the education committees of the Senate and the House of Representatives. Additionally, we surveyed the main print media in the country, and studied E2020's web presence, focusing on its websites and its Facebook, Twitter and YouTube accounts, between November 2010 and August 2011.

This chapter is divided into eight sections. Following the introduction, there is a theoretical discussion on the use of information and communication technologies (ICTs) in the political arena We discuss the results and limitations of two decades of research in the field and propose an analysis that overcomes "technological idealism". The third and fourth sections provide a context for understanding citizen participation in Chile, together with a picture of current debates and the players involved in the field of education. Finally, E2020's appearance in 2008 is described, focusing on the early contacts established with political authorities and the manner by which citizen interest was successfully raised via the internet. The sixth section studies the use the movement has made of the internet to contact citizens and promote their initiatives while the seventh describes and explains E2020's contacts with members of parliament and government authorities. The final part highlights the main conclusions of our research as well as aspects that might be of interest to social movements and think tanks and to researchers interested in political uses of ICTs.

Finally, we should like to point out that in the text we refer to E2020 variously as an academic group, as a movement and as a foundation. Although these three concepts are not synonymous, they reflect the complex character of an organisation like E2020 that presents itself to authorities and citizens in the light of this triple-identification. The three categories are also pertinent because they show how the group evolved over our two-year research period.

INTERNET, POLITICS AND PARTICIPATION

From the nineties on, the incorporation of ICTs into the field of politics has been followed with great interest both by activists and academics studying communications policies, relationships between the state and society, citizen participation and the state of democracy. At first there were many theoretical studies marked with stubborn idealism that insisted that ICTs, and especially the internet, would become the main step forward in increasing the level and quality of public information, offering possibilities for citizens to participate in discussions concerning public affairs (Davis 2001:8). Hopes were set on improving the quality of democracy and on achieving a fully deliberative democracy.

From the theory of democratization to questions raised by evidence

One of the central problems of the optimistic literature about ICTs lies in its attempts to understand ICTs' influence on politics, without accounting for the issues that are central to politics, state action and the dynamics inherent to the discussion of public policies.

The initial debate on ICTs was centred on their potential for democratization. It was assumed that incorporating ICTs would automatically broaden democracy by increasing communication channels, reducing the time taken by the authorities to respond to citizens' queries, and making citizens' opinions more visible. As a result the necessary conditions for a deliberative democracy would be created, the primary condition being a rational discussion on policies related to social coexistence (Jensen 2003: 30).

This first phase of the discussion on the relationship between internet and policies was dominated by political idealism, and based on technological determinism that believed that technology alone was sufficient to start the process of democratization (Costafreda 2004: 4).

These positions were superseded by the empirical evidence of later research. The results of several studies warned that the promises of better democracy through the use of technologies were not being fulfilled, except perhaps in Scandinavian countries (Castells 2000: 177; Costafreda 2004: 4-5). Instead, what these studies showed was that technology did not trigger any radical change. On the contrary, traditional political practices survived the arrival of technology (Parvez 2006: 79).

Although ICTs have been used by governments, parliaments, political parties and professional politicians as a means of establishing unidirectional contact with citizens (Colombo 2006, Smith and Wester 2004, Seaton 2005, Setälä and Grönlund 2006; Araya and Barría 2008, 2009 and 2010; Araya, Barría and Campos 2009), it is important to not only focus on the use of technology, but also on basic issues such as the specific characteristics of political systems and the use of theoretical models of democracy (Martí 2008).

Revisiting various issues to understand the influence of social actors using ICTs on public policies

One thing to bear in mind is that not every social actor can influence politics in the same way. They differ in the type of political resources at their disposal and their ability to use them to influence other players (Dahl 1985: 48-51).

These resources are important because they represent the importance of an actor or social group, and for this reason their type and quality become factors of advantage or disadvantage for players hoping to take part in public policy discussion processes (Kingdon 2003: 51-53).

Some resources are more useful than others in enabling social groups to exert successful pressure on the political system (Pasquino 1989). In the first place, the size of the group, i.e., the number of people in it, counts. Also, the degree of representativeness it has and the extent to which it is recognized by the state in the sector it claims to represent (for example, workers, students, field workers) count too. Another key resource is the money available for an organisation's campaigns, to hire consultants or for media advertising, although these days a functional website and a team to manage the group's virtual presence can substantially reduce costs. A fourth resource, the capacity actors have to formulate proposals, is a central issue when seeking to influence policies. Finally, the group's positioning in the policy process or the political system is a key resource. Other resources can be added to this list, such as the political contacts a group may have, or its relationship with political parties (Valenzuela 1991). In a best-case scenario, a group can become a relevant player to the point that its support for a particular policy may be a prerequisite for the policy's success (Deutsch 1976).

Although this perspective is useful to understand actors' capacities, it does not fully explain why the state pays attention to some and not others; it also leaves out issues, such as the social class origins of an organisation, or state-exercised violence against certain groups and ideas. From a pluralist perspective it would seem that everything depends on resources and expertise. However, this leaves aside the fact that the state is not a neutral player; on the contrary, it takes clearly differentiated stances towards social actors, their strategies and their discourses.

Another point of view, the so-called state-centric perspective developed in the 1980s, makes a final point that we will consider in this study. The state, when taking a position against a social group, is able to manage this difference through various actions, cutting off access to resources, or creating or recognising new social groups whose interests oppose movements that clash with the state (Nordlinger 1981).

This section has rejected the idealistic perspective that saw the incorporation of ICTs in politics as automatically a means to increase levels of democracy and participation. On the contrary, our view is that it is necessary to understand the use of the technologies, incorporating classic topics such as the participation of social groups, and the ways and means the state may create spaces for them. Very probably, the extensive use of the internet will not be highly useful for influencing policy unless it is supported by a movement with a large number of members, representative of certain sectors, or has the capacity to formulate proposals. We should also understand that social movements, and other actors are not only a part of policy discussions because of the weight they carry with society, although this is relevant, but also because of how they relate to the state and the doors that are opened or closed to them by the state.

CITIZEN PARTICIPATION IN POLICY DEVELOPMENT IN CHILE, 1990-2008

Above we showed that the way ICTs work is influenced by the context into which they are inserted. This section will present the forms citizen participation has taken in the public policy arena in Chile between 1990 and 2010. Specifically, we describe the state's attitude vis-à-vis citizens, and how the latter have undergone a process leading to their reactivation from 2000 on.

In the 1990s social demands were moderated in order to not to put too much pressure on the newly reinstated democracy. In this situation the Chilean state was willing to establish contacts with various actors in the policy arena, but these interactions were limited and did not typically develop into open discussions. In other words, the state offered possibilities for community input into specific areas of specific policies, but did not allow real discussion to take place (Delamaza 2009).

Additionally, the list of issues to be considered was reduced: anything outside the institutional framework of Chile's market economy would not be discussed. As well, the discussion preceding the policy formulation stage was based on purely technical arguments using technocratic language. This is evidenced in the relevant literature showing the increasing technocracy of post-dictatorship Chilean governments (Silva 2008), reaching a high point during the Bachelet government (2006-2010), when the committees whose role it was to propose policies were no longer made up of social organizations and authorities but of highly-qualified economists (Aguilera, 2007; Araya, Barría and Drouillas, 2012). As a result, political discussions became centred on specific technical issues. In this context, Chilean think tanks, institutions with headquarters, specialized staff, administrative staff and tangible resources used for operations, were able to participate.

On the other hand, civil-society social groups, unable to sustain a technical discourse, especially quantitatively, were left out of discussions with the state (Márquez 2010). However, new organisations have appeared over the last decade and although they do not have significant resources at their disposal, they have used the internet to form networks, to organise meetings and debates, and to disseminate proposals or research results. The clearest example of this is *Expansiva*, a centre through which academics from universities in Chile and the United States joined forces and, through their website and seminars, gained visibility to the extent that they were a principal resource for President Michelle Bachelet when she formed her first cabinet in 2006.

To all this we should add that Chile, at least until half way through the 2000s, underwent a process of citizen depoliticization. This was reflected in the 1997 parliamentary elections, marked by a low participation and a high number of spoiled and blank votes. From the mid-2000s on this depoliticization gradually gave way to reactivation in the social arena as well as the loss of credibility by politicians (Luna 2008). As a result, social claims were collected by citizens directly, under the slogan "the people united go forward without parties" in 2011. One of the first expressions along these lines was the national strike organized by the Central Workers' Union in 2003, the first action of this kind since the return to democracy (Araya, Barría and Drouillas, 2009).

Citizen reactivation was not restricted to labour movements. Many sectors and interests formed social organizations. In the past few years, for example, organisations of mortgage holders and groups of environmentalists opposing the building of power plants have appeared as well as regional movements in opposition to central government policies towards their respective regions. During 2010 and 2011, Sebastián Piñera's government had to deal with strikes, marches and traffic blockades in cities as far from the capital as Calama, Dichato and Punta Arenas.

Workers were therefore rejecting the 70s-style institutionality (Araya, Barría and Drouillas, 2009) and this also applied to the social sphere where this social reactivation was clearest: the field of education.

THE EDUCATION SECTOR, SOCIAL ACTORS AND ACTION IN THE 2000s

This section will not summarize the education policy of the last twenty years, since several available publications already do so (Mizala 2011; Valenzuela et al. 2008; Picazo 2010). What is intended is to point out certain factors to show how the reactivation process described took shape in the field of education.

The Chilean educational system underwent radical reform in the early '80s. The principal measures taken were: 1) decentralization of state schools, the control of which was moved from the Ministry of Education to the municipalities; 2) a means of financing education by subsidizing all students, including those in private institutions, was established; 3) standardized tests began to be used to measure student achievement; 4) changes were made in how the teaching profession was regulated (Mizala 2007).

These measures, aligned with the neoliberal policies of Pinochet's dictatorship, were maintained after democracy was reinstated in 1990 by successive *Concertación*[1] governments who were focused on extending the system's coverage and on responding to teacher union demands by establishing the Teachers' Statute (the legal framework governing contractual relationships between teachers and schools), and raising teachers' salaries. Also, a number of performance measuring mechanisms were implemented, such as teacher evaluations.

The Chilean educational system was governed by the Teaching Act for almost twenty years (1990-2009) until it was replaced by the General Education Act, based on the principle of freedom of education. Basic education became the families' responsibility and the state's duty was to ensure that it was available for free to ensure access for all (Valenzuela et al. 2008:134). The Ministry of Education is the head of this system and establishes policies, transfers funds and performs control functions.

Education in Chile is organised by level. The first two are compulsory: primary education which lasts eight years and secondary education lasting four. There are three kinds of

---

1 The *Concertación* was a coalition of 17 political parties that governed Chile from the end of the dictatorship in 1990 until it was defeated at the polls by *Renovación Nacional* in 2010.

institutions: municipal schools, where education is free and funds come from state subsidies for each student; the so-called private-subsidized schools, where funding is provided jointly by tax contributions and families; and private schools, with only private funding (Ibidem: 33).

The third level is tertiary education, both technical and professional. At this level, there are institutions that receive public funding, mainly the state universities, and others such as the Technical Education Centres (TEC), institutes and universities, which are privately funded. The state provides public institutions with fixed sums from tax contributions and also provides scholarships for qualifying students in public or private institutions. State contributions received by public institutions are not sufficient to cover costs, forcing them to adopt self-financing policies resulting in high annual fees.

Problems in the Chilean educational system

The Chilean educational system faces a number of problems. The first is its variable quality. In the primary and secondary levels, its structure has contributed to a high degree of segregation, which in practice means that different social classes do not mingle in schools. The municipal schools cater to children from the most vulnerable classes.

Additionally, the tests used to measure teaching quality, such as the SIMCE examination, reveal a wide gap in student performance among the different kinds of institutions. This has led a number of specialists to maintain that the system is responsible for a situation whereby municipal schools will always produce lower performance, while the highest performance will always be found in private schools (Picazo 2010: 75).

Social actors in the field of education

Problems in education not only fuel discussions among specialists in the field, but also among the main social actors in the field. This includes the Teachers' Association, an organization with over 100,000 members and that is more like a union than a professional association. From the 90s, they have been very active in their opposition to the policy of making municipalities responsible for education, in fighting for salary increases, and in demanding more opportunities for professional development (Mizala 2007: 10-11).

A second key actor is the Chilean Student Confederation (CONFECH), which brings together the student federations of the so-called traditional universities, mainly state and Catholic universities. Their demands include strengthening public education, increasing direct state contribution to university budgets (in order to lower university fees and, ultimately, to achieve free university education), as well as democratising universities.

The third player is the secondary school student movement which, unlike secondary school teachers and university students, did not play an active role between 1990 and 2005 (Torres 2010). However, since 2006, they have played a key role, in particular because of their concern for the low quality of their education, especially in the public education system.

Open issues

Towards the end of 2005, secondary school students began to mobilize, demanding, among other things, the elimination of the municipally run public education model, in their view responsible for the differences in the quality of education. In 2006, they moved for a free university entrance exam, and also for extending their low-cost public transport benefits. Later, with widespread citizen support and the support of organizations such as the Teacher's Association and CONFECH, mobilizations concentrated on ending municipal responsibility for education, repealing the law, and improving the quality and strength of state education (De la Cuadra, 2007).

These protests forced the Minister of Education to resign, and by midyear a presidential advisory council for quality in education was formed. Students, education experts, academics, religious authorities and government officials were invited to take part. A report was presented with policy proposals focused on repealing the Teaching Act and passing the General Education Act as well as on the question of quality education (later reports would focus on these same issues). In connection with this, several laws were passed in the last two years, such as the General Education Act creating an Education Supervision Office and the Quality Agency among others, establishing certification mechanisms and creating incentives especially for socio-economically vulnerable sectors. The focus on quality had been an objective for policies dating from the 1990's on (Mizala 2007), but other key demands of the 2006 student movement, such as taking responsibility for education away from the municipalities and strengthening public education were not considered within the policy debate because they were not on the *Concertación* governments' education reform agenda.

An issue that is now part of the accepted state discourse on education is related to human resources and education. In recent years, an argument gaining traction considers that the quality of education depends on what goes on in the classroom, so that teaching results depend on key issues such as teacher training and not so much on socio-economic factors (Eyzaguirre and Fontaine 2008). Thus, issues such as obtaining the best teachers, being able to eliminate the legal restrictions that make it difficult to fire "bad teachers," and establishing a teacher evaluation mechanism, become focal points of this approach, which led to tension between successive governments and the Teacher's Association (Mizala 2007:40-41), as some political players criticized the union for demanding salary increases but not accepting evaluation.

EDUCACIÓN 2020 BREAKS INTO THE FIELD OF EDUCATION

2008 was a year of conflict in Chilean education. Issues discussed in the 2006 demonstrations were still the focus of discussion in social and political spheres, and high school students mobilized once again as there was still no response to their demands. Also, Congress forced the resignation of the Minister of Education following an accusation of corruption, while the Teacher's Association protested against the ministry's teacher evaluations and called for the recognition of an outstanding debt dating from the time schools moved from central to municipal responsibility, two decades earlier (Mizala, 2007).

Within this context, in August 2008, an opinion column was published in the influential political magazine *Qué Pasa*, entitled "Teachers' Statute: A tragedy worse than the Transantiago." The article, written by Mario Waissbluth, denounced the impact the "Teachers' Statute" would have on the quality of education. The article claimed that, even if a teacher was bad, it would be very difficult to fire him or her because the statute did not allow it. The headline was provocative as the tragedy it was forecasting would be worse than the implementation of a new public transport system in Santiago in 2007, widely seen to have been a disaster.

Who wrote the column? Mario Waissbluth is a chemical engineer who graduated from the Universidad de Chile and holds a postgraduate degree in engineering from the University of Wisconsin. In 2008 he was a professor in the industrial engineering department of the Universidad de Chile, teaching public administration. Waissbluth is not a traditional academic;

on the contrary, he has combined academic work with his experience in public administration, especially in connection with new technologies, and also in the private sector. He is well-known in the political sphere, where his expert capacity in public administration is recognized. For these reasons, during the twenty years of Concertación governments (1990-2010), and because of his affinity with the coalition, he was a board member for public entities such as the National Copper Corporation (CODELCO) and the Consejo de Alta Dirección Pública, a high-level advisory council to the president and cabinet.

It was not a coincidence that the article dealt with teacher issues –there was an ongoing discussion on the subject taking place in political and academic circles. Since 2005 Waissbluth had been leading the so– called Public Innovation Club, a discussion group that brought together academics and public administrators to discuss policy and public administration issues. Education was one of the subjects most frequently dealt with at club meetings. The conclusions of these discussions held that the main problem with the quality of Chilean education was the low standards of teachers and head teachers.

Waissbluth's article had immediate effect, reflected in virtual forum discussions held by engineering students of the Universidad de Chile and in the mass media, and soon Waissbluth was invited to present his ideas on education on the most influential political debate programme on Chilean television, *Tolerancia Cero* (Zero Tolerance). He accepted the invitation under the condition that he appear as a representative of a larger group and be accompanied on the programme by students from the School of Engineering of the Universidad de Chile and the Pontificia Universidad Católica de Chile.

Educación 2020 was born with a publication entitled *Manifiesto de Educación 2020*, a document that denounced the "educational disaster" the country was facing and the low standards of teaching staff and head teachers and that called for a national agreement on education where key issues such as a more flexible Teachers' Statute, and an increase in public spending on education were priorities. The manifesto proposed that measures should be taken to ensure that by 2020, the education received by the poorest 20% of the population would be of equal quality to that of the richest 20%.

E2020's strategy

The new movement created a website and a Facebook group with the idea of getting as many citizens as possible to sign on to the manifesto, and then to present the list of supporters to the authorities to demonstrate the public support for their proposals. The initial idea was for a two week campaign and during the first week 15,000 people signed on. Events moved quickly and public reaction was supportive of Waissbluth and his collaborators. They exploded into the media and social networks, and were received by the House of Representatives' Education Committee.

In the following weeks, press coverage continued. E2020 disseminated its proposals widely, which explains in part their rapid and constant presence in newspapers, radio and television. In this context, and only a month after they appeared on scene, E2020 was able to arrange a meeting with the Minister of Education, Mónica Jiménez. At that meeting the ministry's authorities told the movement's representatives that they felt it important that E2020 continue with its course of action and that it should focus on presenting them with proposals.

The E2020 document also had social repercussions. Supporters appeared in several Chilean cities where they organized local groups named after the movement. Waissbluth and his collaborators initially recognized the groups and involved them in discussions of new proposals. However, things changed shortly after, in part because those leading the groups had problems formulating proposals and because their proposals were not considered to be of a high enough standard.

After becoming an "explosive web movement" as the newspaper *El Mercurio* put it, the E2020 founding group decided to make the initiative permanent, to further develop their website and to create a foundation. This decision was taken to create an institutional framework, required to support the work the movement was carrying out, as well as to obtain the necessary infrastructure and financial and human resources. E2020 was successful and two months after it first made its appearance it were installed in furnished offices thanks to the School of Engineering of the Universidad de Chile, and support from private companies. Prolam, an advertising agency, contributed a strategic-positioning plan while Imaginación, a consultancy owned by Enrique Correa (an ex-minister of state from the early 90's and one of the principal lobbyists in the country), offered their communications services (*El Mercurio* 24/12/2008).

E2020 thus became a centre for policy proposals, but it never abandoned the idea that it was a social movement. In fact, at that time Waissbluth defined the group as a social movement and asked citizens for their support in exerting pressure on authorities (*La Tercera* 25/11/2008; 23/3/2009). At the same time, upon becoming a foundation the decision was made to establish a board made up of members with political contacts both on the right and left, people experienced in matters of education, people from the entrepreneurial sector, in addition to Waissbluth and four of the original group members (*El Mercurio* 29/3/2009; *La Tercera* 23/4/2009). They appointed Adriana Delpiano as executive director, a Partido por la Democracia (PPD) leader, who from 1994 to 2008 had been mayor of Santiago, Minister for the Women's National Service, Minister of National Assets and Under-secretary for Regional Development. With this board of directors, and by naming Delpiano as executive director, the idea was to make it possible to open doors in spheres involved with policy decisions.

In 2009, E2020 published a document titled *Se acabó el recreo* (Recess is over), its roadmap for 2009-2020. This broadened the *Manifiesto de Educación 2020*, continuing with the issue of quality of teachers and head teachers and adding concern for other issues including how to finance its proposals. The foundation distributed the document among the presidential candidates for that year's election, presenting then-President Michelle Bachelet with a copy at the Government Palace (*El Mercurio* 24/4/2009).

From the sources used in this section, it is clear that the milestones in the development of the movement were covered by *El Mercurio* and *La Tercera*, the most important newspapers in the country. This indicates that before E2020 was one year old, it was recognised as an actor in the education field, both on the web, where it continued to carry out activities that increased the enormous initial support of citizens, as well as within the political sphere and the media.

E2020 ON THE INTERNET

In the previous section we showed that the internet played an important role in E2020's development as an actor in the field of education, making it possible to mobilise support. In the beginning, the internet was used as an instrument for communication to link a large number of people. This led to the decision to use it as a preferred space for engaging in strategic actions. Later, when the foundation was formed, sufficient resources were allocated to establish a powerful website.

What the E2020 members had in mind was to explore the potential to use online communication to create communities to discuss education-related matters, to carry out surveys on various subjects and to disseminate information through videos. In the following section we will describe how these ideas came to be implemented through specific uses of websites and applications.

www.educacion2020.cl

E2020's online presence began at www.educacion2020.cl. The original idea was to set up a website for two weeks during which people could adhere to the manifesto and then to send the list of names to the authorities. Following the massive support received and the decision to convert the group into a permanent entity the website necessarily became more complex. Today the movement uses its website in a number of ways.

In the first place, the original aim of attracting supporters is maintained. A main feature of the site is that it disseminates information. Documents on public policies written by its members are published, videos of speeches given by members are uploaded, there is a section on E2020 news and education, and a list of frequently asked questions to help understand the foundation's proposals.

The website has a section for discussion forums revolving around Chilean education in general as well as specific proposals and topics connected with E2020 documents and campaigns. The forum section is open enough to allow users outside the group to start a discussion or to publish their own contributions such as surveys. These forums allow for contact between E2020 and supporters, but they are not designed for decision-making on policy proposals.

Initially the idea for the site was for people to add their names to a list of supporters, but other forms of collaboration were incorporated, such as volunteer work, "urban activism", such as street campaigns to get more people to sign on to the manifesto, and virtual activism, using platforms such as Facebook and Twitter to gain support for E2020's proposals.

Twitter

Although the website responded to initial needs, as time passed limitations appeared. The idea of creating online communities proved difficult and Twitter was adopted as an alternative, mainly because it is possible to establish more fluid communication, making it possible, as E2020's social media director has put it, to get a "feeling" for what people think about proposals.

Using *@Educacion2020*, the foundation is able to communicate fluidly with its over 60,000 followers. There are daily messages on weekdays, with one person responsible for this as well as management of E2020's website. As an example of Twitter activity, let us consider two randomly chosen days: on May 2nd 2011 there were 16 messages and on 22 August of the same year, 17. The foundation is thus able to communicate views, to inform followers of activities, to disseminate information on education-related subjects or the views of other players in the sector, and also to maintain a "conversation" with supporters. This is the dialogue format E2020 used in 2010 to start a debate on education (*La Tercera* 7/10/2010).

Facebook

E2020 also uses other internet services, such as Facebook. The first group quickly outgrew Facebook's 5,000-member limit, forcing E2020 to replace it with a Facebook page, where support is expressed through the "like" feature. According to E2020's social director, although Facebook is still used, there are clear limitations, such as the limited discussion options available.

E2020 used Facebook to launch theme campaigns, such as *No more negotiating over Pedagogy*, centred on the insufficient teacher training offered by private universities and professional institutes. This had been a key issue for the movement from the beginning, and the demand was for teachers to take a compulsory certification test before being permitted to work at schools. The campaign organizers promised to collect all Facebook comments on the matter and, like the campaign which originated the group, present them to the relevant authorities (*La Tercera* 27/4/2010).

YouTube

Another channel used by E2020 is YouTube. The foundation uploads videos of its advertising campaigns, video messages sent by members and television programmes its leaders have participated in. There are fewer YouTube users than for the other modalities: near the end of August 2011 there were 208 subscribers and the videos had been viewed 7,901 times. It would appear that the role is secondary, more a place to store videos than to interact with people. This becomes understandable, as both Twitter and Facebook have a person who manages them, answering comments and creating content, while YouTube videos are hardly commented on at all, and comments by users go unanswered.

www.entusmanos.cl

The difficulties encountered at the E2020 website when trying to create online communities were not addressed only with Twitter and Facebook. In addition to these, the decision was taken to create a new website –www.entusmanos.cl– in order to incorporate the community-building applications which were not used on the main site. This second site had a clear aim: to become "the site for Educación 2020 citizen activism." As we show below, the site clearly reflected E2020's characteristics and the kind of relationship expected from its followers. In this sense, it affirms the belief that "informed, empowered citizens

can and must exert pressure for changes in Chilean education."
In a call to citizens, the foundation indicates that this can be
achieved in the following ways:

"1. Obtaining information on news relevant to education; when
citizens are informed and aware of the state of our education
they will be able to demand change.

2. Carrying out various actions to disseminate information
relevant to education and E2020 proposals.

3. Joining E2020, a citizen movement with over 70,000
supporters who seek to improve the quality and equity of
education through changes in public policies for education."

The site was organized into three sections:

1. *Find Out* is devoted to communicating matters of interest
   for citizens about education, which can be followed on the
   same site, or RSS, Facebook or Twitter.

2. *Act* brings together several resources available to E2020
   supporters. First there are three manuals. Two of them,
   produced by UNICEF, seek to guide parents raising children
   from the ages of 4 to 14 and to help them prepare for
   sending their children back to school after the holidays. The
   third has information for students entering university for
   the first time. The second type of resource is a collection
   of available online media and the third features information
   gathered from twelve non-state organizations acting in the
   field of education, including information on their projects
   and links to their websites.

3. *Join* describes E2020 as a citizen movement seeking
   to change education policies. Joining E2020 is defined
   as demonstrating "symbolic support" to the proposals
   contained in the document *Se acabó el recreo*. To join a
   person has to fill out a form providing personal information
   for E2020's database.

Citizen campaigns using various means of communication

The foundation gained access to various communication channels thanks to *pro bono* work and free advertising supplied by agencies, communications consultants and the press.

In 2009, for example, activities were not restricted to the internet. In May, E2020 launched a television campaign (*El Mercurio* 25/5/2009: *La Tercera* 23/6/2009); in January another campaign funded by the Football Channel, a pay-per-view channel broadcasting only professional football (*La Tercera* 29/1/2010). These campaigns were interesting for two reasons: they showed the growth of an organization able to present its proposals in the most important media in the country after only one year on the internet; and secondly, they demonstrated E2020's capacity to obtain resources from other organizations. The campaigns were organized by an advertising agency working *pro bono*, and the spots shown by television channels were free of charge too. In the Football Channel campaign, two players from the national Chilean team took part.

In its first year the foundation carried out other promotional activities. Among these were a number of urban activism activities, putting E2020 volunteers in the streets, especially in places with a lot of traffic and pedestrian circulation. In August 2009, a new membership campaign was launched, enrolling 400 new members. Also, an advertising campaign was carried out both on the underground and in the streets in the capital.

Although E2020 did not function solely online, the foundation used the web as its preferred means of communication. For example, in 2009 www.educacion.cl was used to call for volunteers to help the groups E2020 had organised in various Chilean cities. An online survey was used to find whether people agreed with the various initiatives the foundation was engaging in and in December 2009 an online campaign sought ideas for the 2010-2014 agenda. Additionally, a campaign was held for citizens to put pressure on members of parliament so they would support a budget increase for education. E2020 did this by providing contact information of members of Parliament, including their telephone numbers and their Facebook and Twitter accounts.

There were more internet campaigns in 2010. Together with the launch of www.entusmanos.cl, described above, E2020 called for support for the Ministry of Education's work in the post-earthquake context. Communications in Chile were not working properly, preventing the central government from reaching the whole country. The Ministry needed to evaluate the conditions of school buildings in the sixth and the eighth regions. At www.educacion2020.cl/escuelas, E2020 offered a map showing the locations of schools, and the Ministry form to fill out with information on damage to buildings. The idea was that people could print the form, check the schools and send the completed form to E2020 who would then send it on to the Ministry of Education (*La Tercera* 4/3/2010). The campaign was not as successful as had been expected because not many people got involved and those who did were received with suspicion by the schools' maintenance staffs.

Recently, E2020 started a new campaign to raise funds for the foundation. It was the first time in two years that people were asked for a financial contribution. The fund-raising is carried out online using a platform belonging to the National Treasury. Use of the platform was obtained, free of charge, thanks to political contacts of E2020's leaders.

Staff and activities carried out to maximize internet use

The importance of internet for E2020 is reflected in the various resources assigned by the foundation to work on the website. There is a team of three people whose job is to "position the brand" on internet. The team is made up of a press manager, a digital editor and a person who manages E2020's Twitter and Facebook presence. One of their main aims is to preserve "member loyalty" by keeping in constant contact with E2020's supporters through newsletters and by answering all online queries or comments.

The team also studies the online activities of other non-state organizations. In recent months, the social director has been researching international studies on the use of internet by social movements, especially in terms of Facebook and Twitter followers. Based on these results, they judge whether the use made by E2020 is as effective as possible or if they need to further develop their online activities.

As a result of the comparisons, the team came to the conclusion that Facebook was not being fully exploited, as the number of followers was smaller than that of other organizations. A new campaign was launched to resolve the matter: *No more negotiating over Pedagogy.* However, it does not appear to have been very successful, given that only 2,900 people had joined by September of 2011, fewer than those already following on Facebook.

E2020 also allocates financial resources to improve the use it makes of the web. At present it is paying the costs of using software to check whether their mass mailings are opened and by whom. This is a useful tool for the foundation, providing percentages of opened mail, and also allowing for new actions to be taken, such as resending unopened messages.

FROM INTERNET TO THE POLITICAL SPHERE?

In this section we shall be looking at the way contacts between E2020 and the players in Chilean political institutions developed, to see how the movement followed through on its commitments in government spheres. We will also look at whether this was due to E2020's internet presence or other factors, such as personal political contacts. To find out, we studied the way the movement is perceived by members of congress and government officials, as well as its impact on the ongoing debate on education.

Educación 2020's relationship with the Ministry of Education and Congress

As noted above, Waissbluth's article, the starting-point for E2020, was published on August 21, 2008 in *Qué Pasa*. On September 16 the founding members met with the House of Representatives' Education Committee, who invited them to present their proposals. Following the session, members of congress agreed to "formally support *Educación 2020*'s proposal" and to organize a number of seminars to discuss the specific issues presented. A few weeks later it was the Minister of Education herself, Mónica Jiménez, who received them to discuss the project and exchange ideas. These contacts continued after the movement was launched. On March 11, 2009 the Senate's Education Committee expressed interest in the subject and invited Mario Waissbluth to give a talk on the subject. That same year President Michelle Bachelet met with E2020 representatives.

These were not protocol meetings; rather, they show that E2020 achieved recognition as an actor with something to say about education. For this reason, in 2009 and 2010, Mario Waissbluth and other E2020 leaders were invited by the education committees of both congressional chambers, to present his views on the bills seeking to create a national system to ensure quality education at preschool, primary and secondary school levels. This bill would introduce innovative measures regarding per student subsidies paid to public and subsidized schools. Also in 2009, the foundation participated in the parliamentary committee debating the Ministry of Education's budget.

To sum up, between 2008 and 2010, E2020 took part in six of the sessions on education held by of the Chamber of Representatives and by the Senate. This participation is relatively low, given the 36 sessions held by the Representatives' Education Committee in 2009, in addition to 46 sessions held by the Senators. E2020 was present at the sessions as one of several players discussing specific subjects and had received official support for its proposals. For example, in several sessions, E2020 members were considered as experts. Additionally, at the sessions both before and after those they had been especially invited to attend, several non-E2020 researchers in education policies were also present. This leads us to question the weight the movement actually brings to bear on the issues debated in parliament.

As well as the contacts made at the committees on education, E2020 communicates fluidly with members of parliament, a result of earlier work carried out by the foundation. They have a legal advisor who regularly attends the sessions of both Representatives and Senators and reports to E2020 staff. The foundation has always managed to hold meetings with political parties with elected representatives, to contact members of parliament via e-mail and to send technical reports as input to parliamentary discussions.

From the interest in E2020 taken by the executive branch when Bachelet was president, we would be justified in thinking that the movement received preferential treatment. For a start, the Minister of Education and the President were willing to meet E2020, and even signed a cooperation agreement. A protocol was drawn up, with four key points: training for heads of schools; a system of grants for teachers' professional studies; certification for professional teaching courses; and reconsideration of the course loads of primary school teachers (*La Tercera* 7/1/2010; *El Mercurio* 8/1/2010; *La Nación* 8/1/2010).

In March 2010, the coalition government in Chile was voted out for the first time since 1990 and the right took over the government after twenty years of Concertación governments. This change may have negatively affected E2020, especially because of the connections Waissbluth and the director of the foundation, Adriana Delpiano, had with the coalition government. The foundation describes how in the first months of the new government, the Minister of Education, Joaquín Lavín, did not meet with E2020 members. Nevertheless, they finally managed to talk to him following pressure resulting from a campaign organised on Twitter.

Explaining how E2020 burst into the debate on education policies

The question as to whether E2020 gained access to decision-making spheres because of its use of the internet is well worth considering, and seems to be confirmed by the Twitter campaign mentioned above. All key players consulted agree that the internet played an important role in positioning E2020 as a key actor in education. Also, members of parliament and of the executive were aware of the impact the movement was achieving online from the beginning.

However, some actors have stated that internet did not play such a key role in positioning E2020 within policy discussion spheres. More likely, they say, it is Mario Waissbluth and his network of contacts that played the key role. For example, the first meetings with the Ministry of Education were made possible by the then Under-secretary for Education, Cristián Martínez, who had been a member of the Public Innovation Club that Waissbluth directed. One member of parliament agrees with this statement. In his opinion, E2020 is part of the debate on education thanks to the fact that Waissbluth was able to tap into pre-existing dissatisfaction regarding education in Chilean society. The legislator goes even further, saying that the committees will only listen to Waissbluth. At E2020, their leader's political contacts and widespread respect are recognized as crucial for their taking part in the debate, but they also underscore the clarity of their message, the advantages of a speaker who can communicate well and the impact of the press and of internet.

Although players in the government and in Congress tend to mark E2020 as one of the less influential players in the field of education, when compared to the principal players in the field (student associations, the Teachers Union and the Chilean Association of Municipalities), it is nevertheless significant that a relatively small association accessed the highest levels of political discussion, and even signed agreements with the Bachelet government. One possible explanation for this achievement may be the fact that political players recognize E2020 as an organization specializing in education policies that provides them with needed inputs when the government seeks to analyse related subjects being discussed in Congress. That is to say, as one interviewee put it, they welcome it as a new research centre providing data and proposals.

CONCLUSIONS: E2020 AND THE DEBATE ON INTERNET AS A MEANS FOR SOCIAL PARTICIPATION

In this paper we have seen how E2020 burst into the Chilean field of education and how it gained visibility as a player in the press and in the political sphere and we analysed how it interacted with the Ministry of Education and Congress. Three main factors are worth focusing on in this closing section. The first is E2020 as a group of experts, its performance and the resources that have allowed it to become a player in the discussion on education in Chile. Later, we shall look at the reasons for their being part of this discussion, with special reference to the use of internet and other explanations. Finally, a broader discussion would look at the contribution this case study makes to the analysis of internet strategies used by other social movements and think tanks.

The group emerged as a temporary association with the objective of proving and platform to support the ideas that

Mario Waissbluth, a well-known academic, was to present on a television programme. E2020 was born with an agenda, the goal of having its proposals reach the relevant authorities. The internet was expressly used to garner support for the agenda.

E2020's tremendous success, demonstrated by the 15,000 who signed on to its proposals in the first week, together with the formal backing it received from the Chamber of Representatives' Education Committee for its proposals, led E2020 to to become a formal organization, thanks to which they were able to receive funds and services. From a movement with an agenda and a group of adherents, it became a foundation, with a board of directors made up of representative spokespersons with access to political networks.

The change meant a more refined use of the internet, which was no longer seen as just a means to capture supporters. From that moment on, it was used as a channel to disseminate the work carried out by E2020 and to obtain support beyond merely signing a form. Volunteer work was encouraged, as was support for campaigns and fundraising. Also, the online strategy was professionalized, thanks to investments in software and the creation of a full time team exclusively focused on expanding the movement's online presence.

E2020's entry into policy discussion spheres resulted from some of the things described in the previous section, such as: Waissbluth being highly regarded in political spheres; the political contacts of E2020 spokespersons; the fact that its issues and the Ministry of Education's policies converged and; the importance the Ministry attributed to dealing with a group with an agenda distinct from the positions of the Teacher's Association. Another key aspect is that E2020 was able to present proposals using technical language and convert them into actionable guidelines. This is relevant in the Chilean context, where policy discussion has become technocratic and social movements without the ability to articulate their arguments in technical terms find themselves isolated in policy debates (Márquez 2010).

If E2020's example can produce some practical conclusions, recommendations or good practices, they are related to the fact that an extensive use of internet to generate public support is not enough to enable social movements to effectively participate in public policy discussions in Chile. On the contrary, this paper has shown how the content of the claims and their relationship with dominant discourses, the capacity to formulate proposals making clear technical contributions to on-going discussion, and the existence of political networks, are all still key factors for success.

This case also shows that the internet is a useful tool for launching a concept into the media and the public spheres and that succeeding in that regard can help obtain additional funds and human resources, all of which will tend to strengthen the structure of the organization and the overall capacity of a social movement.

E2020 was constituted by a group of members of a political and intellectual elite and university graduates with the political and social networks necessary to gain access to policy discussion spheres and who were capable of developing technical proposals that would be favoured by policymakers. The internet did not open channels for citizen participation; but it linked E2020's proposals with people, at the same time giving the proposals a civic dimension. Thanks to its work with the internet, E2020 did not enter public debate solely as a group of intellectuals and experts, but also as a social movement, although it is still not perfectly clear that it is, in fact, a movement.

It would seem, therefore, that the use of the internet and social networks opens up possibilities by which organisations, think tanks and research centres with technically sound policy agendas can seek public support via the internet, achieving a certain citizen-endowed legitimacy for their proposals.

REFERENCES

Aguilera, C. 2007. "Participación Ciudadana en el Gobierno de Bachelet: Consejos Asesores Presidenciales". *América Latina Hoy* 46: 119-143.

Araya, E. and D. Barría. 2008. "Modernización del Estado y Gobierno Electrónico en Chile 1994-2006". *Buen Gobierno* 5: 80-103.

--------------------------. 2009. "E-participación en el Senado Chileno. ¿Aplicaciones Deliberativas?". *Convergencia. Revista de Ciencias Sociales* 52: 239-268.

--------------------------. 2010. *E-Goverment and Citizen Participation in Chile*. In *Politics, Democracy and E-government: Participation and Service Delivery*, edited by Reddick, C. Hershey: IGI Global.

Araya, E., D. Barría and G. Campos. 2009. Internet and Political Parties in Chile. In *Systems Thinking and E-participation: ICT in the Governance of Society*, edited by Córdoba-Pachón, J.R. and A.Ochoa-Arias. Hershey: IGI Global.

Araya, E., D. Barría and O. Drouillas. 2009. *Sindicatos y Políticas Públicas en Argentina, Bolivia, Brasil, Chile y Venezuela. Balance de una Década (1996-2004)*. Santiago: Editorial Universitaria.

Castells, M. 1997. *La Era de la Información. Economía, Sociedad y Cultura. Volumen 2: El Poder de la Identidad*. Madrid: Siglo XXI.

--------------------. 2000. *La Galaxia Internet*. Madrid: Plaza y Janés.

Colombo, C. 2006. "Innovación Democrática y TIC, ¿Hacia una Democracia Participativa?". *Revista de Internet, Derecho y Política* 3: 28-40.

Costafreda, A. 2004. *Determinismo Institucional versus Determinismo Tecnológico: TICs y Representación Política en Chile y España*. Paper presented at Seminario e-governance, Doctorado de Sociedad de la Información, Universidad Oberta de Cataluña.

Dahl, R. 1985. *Análisis Político Actual*. Buenos Aires: EUDEBA.

Davis, R. 2001. "Tecnologías de la Comunicación y Democracia: el Factor Internet". *Cuadernos de Información y Comunicación* 6: 9-32.

De la Cuadra, F. 2007. "Conflicto social, Hipergobernabilidad y Participación Ciudadana. Un Análisis de la 'Revolución de los Pingüinos'". *Polis. Revista de la Universidad Bolivariana* 5 (16).

Delamaza, G. 2009. *Participation and Mestizaje of State-Civil Society in Chile*. In *Widening Democracy. Citizens and Participatory Schemes in Brazil and Chile*, edited by Silva, P. and H. Cleuren. Leiden: Brill.

Deutsch, Karl. 1976. *Política y Gobierno*. México: Fondo de Cultura Económica.

Eyzaguirre, B. and L. Fontaine. 2008. *Las Escuelas que Tenemos*. Santiago: Centro de Estudios Públicos.

Jensen, J. 2003. "Virtual Democratic Dialogue? Bringing together Citizens and Politicians". *Information Polity* 8 (1-2): 29-47.

Kingdon, J. 2003. *Agendas, Alternatives and Public Policies*. New York: Longman.

Luna, J. P. 2008. *Partidos Políticos y Sociedad en Chile. Trayectoria Histórica y Mutaciones Recientes*. In *Reforma a los Partidos Políticos en Chile*, edited by Fontaine, A. et. al. Santiago, Chile: UNDP, CEP, Libertad y Desarrollo, Proyectamerica y CIEPLAN.

Martí, J. L. 2008. "Alguna Precisión sobre las Nuevas Tecnologías y la Democracia Deliberativa y Participativa". *Revista de Internet, Derecho y Política* 6: 3-12.

Márquez, R. 2010. *La 'Medida' de lo Posible: Cuantificación y Esfera Pública en Chile*. PhD Thesis, Universiteit Leiden, Holanda.

Mizala, A. 2007. *La Economía Política de la Reforma Educacional en Chile*. Serie Estudios Socio - Económicos 36, Corporación de Estudios para Latinoamérica (CIEPLAN). Santiago de Chile: CIEPLAN.

Nordlinger, E. 1981. *On the Autonomy of the Democratic State*. Cambridge: Harvard University Press.

Parvez, Z. 2006. "Informatization of Local Democracy: A Structural Perspective". *Information Polity* 11 (1): 67-83.

Pasquino, G. 1989. *Participación Política, Grupos y Movimientos*. In *Manual de Ciencia Política*, compiled by Pasquino, G. Madrid: Alianza Editorial.

Picazo, I. 2010. "La Metamorfosis de la Regulación Pública en la Educación Escolar en Chile: hacia un Estado Post-neoliberal. Pensamiento Educativo." *Revista de Investigación Educacional Latinoamericana* 46 (1): 63-91.

Seaton, J. 2005. "The Scottish Parliament and E-democracy". *Aslib Proceedings* 57 (4): 333-337.

Setälä, M., and K. Grönlund. 2006. "Parlamentary Websites: Theoretical and Comparative Perspectives", *Information Polity* 11 (2): 149-162.

Silva, P. 2008. *In the name of reason. Technocrats and politics in Chile*. University Park: Penn State University Press.

Smith, C., and W. Webster. 2004. "Members of the Scottish Parliament on the Net". *Information Polity* 9 (1-2): 67-80.

Subsecretaría de Transportes (SUBTEL). 2010. "Encuesta Nacional de Consumidores de Servicios de Telecomunicaciones". Available at www.mtt.gob.cl/prontus_mtt/site/artic/20100203/asocfile/20100203144637/encuesta_subtel_2s_2009_prensa.pdf [1-3-2012].

Torres, R. 2010. *Juventud, Resistencia y Cambio Social: el Movimiento de Estudiantes Secundarios como un 'Actor Político' en la Sociedad Chilena Post-Pinochet (1986-2006)*. Available at halshs.archives-ouvertes.fr/docs/00/49/88/69/PDF/RodrigoTorres.pdf [30-1-2012]

UN (United Nations). 2003. *World Public Sector Report 2003. E-Government at the Crossroads*. New York: United Nations.

Valenzuela, J.M., P. Labarrera and P. Rodríguez. 2008. "Educación en Chile: entre la Continuidad y las Rupturas. Principales Hitos de las Políticas Educativas". *Revista Iberoamericana de Educación* 48: 129-145.

Valenzuela, J. S. 1991. "Labor Movements and Political Systems: A Conceptual and Typological Analysis". *Working Paper* 167 December, The Hellen Kellogg Institute for International Studies, University of Notre Dame.

3. USING WEB 2.0 TO INFLUENCE PERU'S ICT SECTOR

Jorge Bossio

INTRODUCTION

One of the projects conducted under the Impact 2.0 umbrella was Peru's "laboratory" to link research and policy relating to information and communication technology (ICT), a project that experimented with a variety of social networking tools and strategies to link telecommunications research and policy and, more specifically, on the government's initiative to develop a National Broadband Plan for Peru. The research addressed the problems and possibilities involved in using web 2.0 and online social networking tools within an information and advocacy campaign designed to impact the formulation of Peru's broadband policy.

In planning and evaluating the experiment, the Overseas Development Institute's (ODI) Context, evidence and links framework was used (Crewe and Young 2002). It was therefore organized on the basis of the following components: (i) policy context analysis and subject selection; (ii) strategy development and implementation, focusing on the development and use of web 2.0 tools to link scientific evidence with decision-making processes; and (iii) consolidation of the links forged between research networks, activists and policymakers; and finally, (iv) project evaluation.

The intervention sought to influence policies related to information and communications technologies (ICTs) and the first step was to analyze the policy context in Peru (existing policies and laws, relevant actors and institutions, etc.). Next, the specific policy area to attempt to influence was selected: the implementation models for national broadband policies. In addition to the analysis of the specific policy context, a review of research evidence on which the various interested parties sustained their respective positions was conducted.

As will be seen later, the first stage of the strategy was to inform the public of the ongoing debate on the subject within the government. Also, we sought to use ICTs to link the discussions which were part of the debate, such as Peru's Digital Agenda,[1] so that the discussions would not be limited to the work being done by the government-established committee on broadband policy.

Later, the second, more active, stage was implemented. This involved introducing complementary and alternative research-based evidence to the discussions of the various interest groups and government officials.

The final stage of the strategy involved a change of focus: instead of seeking a place where we would be listened to, we offered a place where everyone might present their positions. Thus, while the previous stages had sought to make the issue visible and to introduce alternative evidence, this stage added a series of public activities. This allowed voices to be multiplied and actors who traditionally reject open debates and discussions became interested. This stage included, very importantly, the production of audio-visual materials, the organization of public meetings and active participation in forums and events where matters related to the campaign were discussed.

---

1 The Digital Agenda is a multi-sectoral process for the National Information Society Plan for Peru.

The research process is described in detail below, beginning with analysis of the context as well as a review of the actors involved and the discourses they appropriate and disseminate (Bossio 2010a). Following that, we describe the stages of the adopted strategy and the decisions taken during the ongoing campaign. The final part of the paper reflects upon the social networks' potential to facilitate efforts to influence decision making.

Selecting the policy to be influenced

From the very beginning, we decided to choose one specific ICT policy process which we expected to be developed in 2011. Narrowing the field of policy processes to influence was intended to improve our ability to establish and maintain contacts with all relevant actors from the beginning of the process.

In order to identify the priority ICT policy issues on the government's agenda, we conducted an initial survey of an open group of over eighty experts and professionals in the sector. The results showed that the most important issue being considered by the government in the short-term was the implementation of the broadband backbone network. (Other issues we ultimately discarded included legislation to protect personal information and some issues related to the regulation of mobile telephones, such as pre selection of the international carrier and reduction of interconnection fees).

The Peruvian government had recognized the importance that broadband would have in making the country more competitive, together with its potential to support the country's insertion into a globalized economy and in fostering its economic and social growth.[2] In 2010, the government established a temporary multi-sectoral committee that was mandated to develop a "National plan for the development of broadband in Peru."

---

2 Supreme Decision 063-2010-PCM

The first of the committee's recommendations highlighted the need for "infrastructure and an adequate supply of appropriate services." This recommendation is extremely important, not only because it requires large public and private sector investments, but also because the regulatory and institutional design to accompany the implementation of the infrastructure would determine the model of Peru's future telecommunication market.

The message the campaign sought to transmit focused on the importance of the initial implementation of the broadband backbone network, to contribute academic evidence on the positive and negative aspects of various possible models and also to ensure that empirical evidence informed the final decision.

To understand the central issues in the debate on the implementation of the broadband backbone network, we consulted both civil society and academic experts through group meetings and personal interviews. We also extended an invitation to participate in these conversations to the private sector and the government. They did not respond initially, but both sectors later sought to participate in the forums opened up by our project in order to ensure that their perspectives were also heard.

Telecommunications and broadband in Peru

In the 1990s, Peru, together with other Latin American countries, launched a programme of public services and infrastructure reform. Unlike developed countries, the reform process in Peru had to deal with a number of limitations: insufficient infrastructure; obsolete technology; a scarcity of human resources; little or no information on the situation of the telecommunication companies; a weak financial market; and a fragile legal and institutional framework (Bossio, 2010a). This situation meant that potential investors perceived the ventures as risky and forced the government to provide greater security for investments connected to the awarded contracts (Abdala and Spiller 1999).

In the case of telecommunications, the reform process sought to liberalize the markets and attract the necessary private investment to develop the infrastructure (Barrantes and Pérez 2006). We started to see significant investment in the telecommunications sector by 1994. However, despite the increased investment and the sustained GDP growth over a ten-year period, in 2010 Peru was still lagging regionally in terms of broadband access.[3]

Dominant ideas and alternative evidence: the campaign message

The committee entrusted with designing Peru's broadband plan in 2010 was made up of actors from both the public and private sectors.[4] The committee published three documents during its period of operation: *Analysis of the development of broadband in Peru; Barriers limiting the development of broadband in Peru;* and a document explaining its vision, goals and policy proposals.

According to the committee's analysis, the main factors behind Peru's lagging access to broadband services are: (1) inadequate data transportation networks, particularly of fibre-optic networks; (2) difficulty of deploying access networks (mainly due to municipal regulations and issues concerning the protection of cultural and archaeological heritage); (3)

---

3 The committee shows the results presented in the "Cisco Broadband Barometer 2009" which places Peru last in South America with only 2,9% penetration of broadband services.

4 Public sector: Communications Under-secretary (MTC); director-general of Regulations and International Affairs in Communications (MTC); representative from the National Research and Training for communications Institute (INCITEL); representative from the Presidency of the Ministers Council (National Bureau of Informatics and e-Government); representative of the Supervising Organisation for Private Investments in Telecommunications (OSPITEL). Private sector: representative of the Association for the Advance of National Infrastructure (AFIN).

restrictions in the availability of radio spectrum for mobile broadband; (4) high regulatory costs; (5) limited market competition high concentration; (6) high cost of equipment and telecommunications services; (7) limited production of digital content and applications, including e-government; and finally, (8) people's lack of ability and capacity to take the best possible advantage of broadband potential.

But there is also evidence of other reasons for the gap, such as that most people cannot afford the services, a cause that was highlighted in reports published by the Economic Commission for Latin America and the Caribbean (ECLAC) (Jordan et al. 2010).

To justify the need for broadband planning, the Peruvian government adopted the discourse of multilateral organizations such as the World Bank, and its *Analysis of the development of broadband in Peru* described broadband as an "instrument to dynamize development and competition."[5]

The analysis also cites, as evidence: an ECLAC article (2010), an article from Colombia's Centre for Research in Telecommunications (CINTEL), the results of the Ibero-American Association of Telecommunications Research Centres and Companies (AHCIET-Asociación Iberoamericana de Centros de Investigación y Empresas de Telecomunicaciones) meeting in 2010, and the XIIIth Regulators and Operators' Summit Declaration REGULATEL-AHCIET.

These being the sources used by the committee, it was to be expected that the dominant discourse would follow the lines drawn by the large telecommunications companies, who dominate forums such as CINTEL and AHCIET and use them to strengthen their lobbying.

Regarding the deployment of a fibre-optic broadband backbone network, the prevailing model, generally defended by

---

5 Temporary multi-sectoral committee for the production of the "National Plan for Broadband Development in Peru. Lima: Ministerio de Transportes y Comunicaciones.

telecommunications companies, particularly by the dominant operator, held that the network would be constructed and operated by a private company, based on demand estimation from a private sector perspective. There are risks involved in this model, mainly due to barriers to competition, increased market concentration in data transport services, the time lag in implementing services in remote areas and entry barriers for local and niche operators.

Faced with this discourse, it is clear that the evidence provided by independent sources is not overly abundant. However, recent papers from the Regional Dialogue on the Information Society – DIRSI (Barrantes and Agüero, 2010b) and ECLAC (Jordan et al, 2010) have contributed to knowledge on the subject that the campaign developed by the national laboratory, and that we/they attempted to introduce in order to complement and provide alternatives to the documents produced by the committee, to highlight the need to consider additional factors and to highlight the risks involved in implementing a broadband backbone network based on the dominant discourse.

CONTEXT AND LINKS: THE ACTORS INVOLVED

For the context, evidence and links model, identifying actors in a position to make decisions or exert influence on specific policies is of capital importance. Our next step was therefore to map out the various parties interested in the deployment of broadband network, including relevant public entities, private entities with the capacity to exert influence and civil society groups interested and actively involved in the matter. We identified potential allies among this last group to carry out the campaign. We also tried to establish links among the actors, in terms of power relations and conflicting interests.

The two main actors from the public sector are the regulatory body (OSPITEL) and the Ministry of Transport and Communications

(MTC). OSPITEL was founded in 1991 as part of regulatory reform during the privatization of the telecommunication sector. Its other functions include: promotion of private investment in telecommunications; fostering a climate of free and fair competition; and establishing policies to ensure interconnection among telecommunications operators. The MTC is in charge of establishing telecommunications policies and monitoring their results, issuing and revoking concessions, authorizations, permits and licenses, and administering the use of the radio spectrum, among other tasks.

Another relevant public sector actor is the Agency for the Promotion of Private Investment (ProInversión), in charge of the administration of investment offers for the private sector. Finally, Congress acts through the Committee for Transport and Communications and, to a lesser extent, the Consumer Defence Committee and the Public Services Regulating Bodies, both of which are key actors in the sector, especially for implementing policies requiring legal adjustments. In the multi-sectoral committee referred to above, there were two representatives from the MTC and one from OSPITEL.

Another public entity taking part in the debate (with a representative on the committee, although with limited power), is the National Bureau for e-Government and Informatics (*Oficina Nacional de Gobierno Electrónico e Informática*), which presides over a multi-sectoral committee in charge of follow-up for Peru's Digital Agenda. Several players from the private sector also come into play, with the most influential being the Telefónica group and TELMEX. Telefónica is the dominant operator in all telecommunication markets and TELMEX is an important competitor in mobile telephony and data communication. The companies in the sector use the Association for the Promotion of Infrastructure (AFIN) for joint lobbying efforts. An AFIN member was on the committee.

There are also several academic actors, including the Institute for Peruvian Studies (IEP), which as a member of the DIRSI network disseminates research results, the Economic and Social Research Consortium (CIES) and the Group for Development Analysis (GRADE), More recently, we can add the Peruvian Studies Institute of the San Martín de Porres University to this list. Several consulting firms, including Apoyo Consultoría, DN Consultores and Alterna contributed to the debate within the sector and carry indirect influence when they engage with the media.

Civil society organizations are less influential, not only because of their relative size and capacity, but also because they have not been able to form a common agenda. On the one side, we have consumer associations, the strongest being the Peruvian Association of Consumers and Users (ASPEC). On the other, there is a burgeoning network of activists, the Peru ICT Forum, which brings together NGOs that have implemented ICT development projects, including CEPES (Centro Peruano de Estudios Sociales), Soluciones Prácticas ITDG and Engineers without Borders. Although not always consistently, these organizations have promoted dialogue and reflection on ICT-related subjects involved in the design and implementation of public policies since 2000, when they became involved in preparatory activities for the World Summit on the Information Society.

Finally, it is important to point out that the sources of information used as a basis for sustaining decisions are also actors. Data often comes from studies carried out by international consulting firms, but are often part of research carried out by international agencies such as the International Telecommunications Union, the World Bank, the Inter-American Development Bank and ECLAC. There are also international forums such as the Telecommunications Regulators Forum (REGULATEL), the Inter-American Telecommunications Commission (CITEL), the Andean Committee of Telecommunications Authorities (CAATEL) and the APEC Telecommunications and Information Working Group, whose discussions, reports and agreements influence the Peruvian regulatory agenda. On the private sector side, AHICET and GSMA are the most influential.

71

It is important to point out that, even when the private sector participated in the multi-sectoral committee for the National Broadband Plan, representatives of civil society and academia were absent, making it difficult to influence the process.

THE STRATEGY FOR INFLUENCE

The strategy proposed for the project was based on the work of civil society actors, who, using academic research, were to develop a platform of action and discourse to reach decision makers.

The review of alternative evidence, together with meetings and interviews carried out by a research team of academics and activists resulted in policy briefs. Dissemination of these documents through blogs and social networks was intended to uphold civil society networks to construct specific evidence-based messages and recommendations to influence policymakers.

It is worth pointing out that although using social networking tools was an a priori decision, we never planned to limit our communication to virtual networks. When bringing civil society participants into the campaign, we included an existing network of ICT activists, the Peru ICT Forum.

Intervention time

One of the defining factors to carry out our intervention was that the two first documents developed by the committee were submitted for public consideration and opened to comments in two workshops held in April and June 2010. The committee held a total of forty-two meetings, inviting various actors to many of them, and then published the minutes on their web page, demonstrating a great deal of transparency in their work.

However, despite the many possibilities for participation, the process promoted by the Peruvian "laboratory" to work with civil society networks to influence the policy agenda faced many difficulties.

The first activity was to gather comments on the first draft version of the National Broadband Plan. during a meeting of the research team with representatives of the ICT Forum. A draft document by the researchers was presented and discussed at the meeting, where it was decided to prepare a Google Docs document to be shared by all participants to gather suggestions and recommendations for the committee. The resulting document was sent to the committee's technical secretary via email. Through this project, we also sought to make this mode of cooperation among academics and civil society activists visible through the social networks.

The visibility stage

Although some civil society actors got involved in the preparation of the document mentioned above, participation was less than had been hoped for. So, we decided to open a blog in which each of the specific subjects we had considered at the meeting was displayed as a separate publication, open to comments. The response was low again, so we changed tools again and put together a page using a wiki platform. This tool was not attractive either, so we finally moved onto Facebook, where we created two pages: one for the National Broadband Plan discussion, and another for the Digital Agenda, which had as its first strategy, the implementation of a broadband backbone network. This time we succeeded and the pages were not only used by broader civil society, but also attracted the attention of the multi-sectoral committee, at one meeting leading a committee member to request that civil society members who participated in the debate via social networks should be invited:

"The OSPITEL representative expressed that it would be important to have the opinion of those involved in important discussions on broadband through the internet's social networks (...) in order to ask them to join the next meeting as representatives of civil society, and so listen to their comments and/or contributions to the work being carried out by the Committee."[6]

This was possibly one of the greatest achievements of the pilot projects: gaining visibility for civil society proposals through the use of social networking tools. Nevertheless, it is important to point out that the contents of what had been published and commented on in Facebook was known to committee members until the day of the meeting we were invited to attend. Ironically, committee members had heard about "an interesting debate on Facebook," but were not able to view it because access to Facebook is blocked in government offices in Peru.[7]

Following the committee meeting, we moved to a second phase of the strategy: disseminating the messages to members of society who would be able to exert their influence on the debate.

Dissemination

The second strategic stage we implemented sought to share the message with relevant or potentially relevant actors. At the time, Peru was in a pre-election period, which was considered to be a good moment for the campaign. We reviewed government plans, the proposals presented by the main presidential candidates regarding telecommunications in general, and broadband services in particular, and we participated at meetings held by universities which were seeking to insert issues relating to

6 Minutes of the Multi-sectorial Committee meeting n° 34 are available at www. mtc.gob.pe/portal/proyecto_banda_ancha/ACTA%20REUNION%2034.pdf

7 See chapter 9 in this volume

science and technology into the election debate. Our objective was to learn from, and talk to, the relevant technical advisers of the main political parties. However, our strategy did not work given that the advisers rarely took part in the debates we organized, with the exception of one engineer, Carlos Romero, who had been involved in developing the platform for the Perú Posible party, and with whom we spoke on several occasions.

The project received little attention during the election period, as attention was fixed on other national issues; the authorities, who knew they would not keep their positions following the election, had no motivation to meet to discuss policies that they would have no role in.

The second meeting to coordinate with civil society was thus held after the election of the new government but before the new authorities had been designated or confirmed into their positions. The meeting took place as part of the preparatory process leading to the Forum on Internet Governance, during which a policy document on Latin American models to implement broadband backbone networks (Bossio 2010b) was distributed and discussed. The document referred to the main strategy being discussed by the National Broadband Committee, but the timing was just not right.

The third meeting, held at the beginning of October 2011, took place once the new sectoral authorities had been designated. Both the telecommunications sector (responsible for the National Broadband Plan) and the authorities responsible for the implementation of the Peruvian Digital Agenda approached civil society and academia to present plans, and hear opinions, on the implementation of the network. This was perceived by the actors involved as a positive gesture that signalled a more open position. It was also helpful that there was a degree of continuity: both OSPITEL and the Ministry of Transport and Communication saw the people who had led the process during the previous government be kept on by the new government.

The participation stage

The post-electoral continuity mentioned above was advantageous for the project when implementing the participation stage. At this point, we decided to work through the La Mula news portal, not only because it receives numerous visits (over one million per month), and is one of the 200 most-visited websites in Peru, but also because of the prestige it gained during the election period when 2011 Nobel laureate Mario Vargas Llosa mentioned it in his weekly column for the Spanish daily El País, which also won the prize for Journalism and Human Rights offered by the Peruvian National Coordinator of Human Rights.[8]

La Mula installed an internet television platform during the election period for the use of independent journalists who could not express themselves freely in the media they worked for. Making use of this platform, the national laboratory participated in a software programme called Código Abierto. Many of the key people, who were soon to enter the debate after elections once the ministerial teams had been designated, were invited to take part, as were those from the private sector through the AFIN representative, and several independent experts and members of civil society collectives. The chance to use this public arena to discuss National Broadband Plan contents was welcomed. In fact, members of the committee asked our team to present a special Código Abierto programme to show the plan's scope. This approach succeeded in making the debate visible, and we also succeeded in providing a new incentive to participate.

Tools to exercise influence

One of the laboratory's aims was to evaluate the potential uses of social networking tools and services to influence

---

8 See derechoshumanos.pe/2011/12/ceremonia-de-entrega-de-los-premios-de-derechos-humanos-2011/

telecommunication policy. We thus used several of these tools for the campaign in order to determine the best scenarios for debates and to spread ideas that differed from those expressed in the dominant discourse.

At first, we planned to use Facebook and Twitter, as their use was increasingly widespread. According to Social Bakers,[9] the number of Facebook accounts in Peru rose from 5 to nearly 8 million in the first half of 2011, when it was being used for strategic political marketing during the municipal elections at the end of 2010 and for the presidential and Congress elections in April and June of 2011. Facebook was also used by groups of citizens to organize around particular issues during the elections.

Twitter is also used widely by journalists and activists, with about 255,000 users in mid-2011. The most well-known case of Twitter use in Peru was citizens' call for more information about the events taking place in Bagua, where indigenous people had been forcefully repressed by the police. Twitter was also important during the electoral debates.[10]

However, these tools did not have the impact we had anticipated in numerical terms. This is why we decided to move to internet television and a "niche strategy" regarding our target public, and increasing our output with quality content. We found that audio-visual material fulfilled both objectives as it was (i) more attractive to our target public than written messages, and (ii) it was attractive to interviewees, who readily accepted our invitations to participate.

The prestige of La Mula's portal was also an important contribution because it lent credibility to our communications and helped to attract relevant actors to the debate on telecommunication policy. The Código Abierto programme ran seven live interview and discussion programmes about National

---

9 See www.socialbakers.com/facebook-statistics/peru

10 See the report prepared by the daily La República at www.larepublica.pe/13-05-2011/twitter-peru-y-sus-trend-topics-mundiales

Broadband Plan, featuring researchers such as: Aileen Agüero from IEP; Wilmar Pebe, a member of the committee that drafted the platform of the Partido Nacionalists Nationalist Gana Perú, and of the transition committee of the MTC; Juan Pacheco, general manager of AFIN; experts such as Carlos Huamán, Executive Director for DN Consultores; and Geoffrey Cannock, Member and Applied Economics Manager for the consultant firm, Apoyo.

As we pointed out earlier, the debate came to the attention of the committee members, who came to the programme in order to explain that the National Broadband Plan passed in the final days of Alan García's government. Participants were Patricia Carreño, Regulations and International Affairs Director General for the MTC; Luis Pacheco, Vice Manager for Research in Competence and Regulatory Policies at OSPITEL; and the Vice Minister for Communications, Raúl Pérez-Reyes.

This strategy was further strengthened by the use of Facebook and Twitter in addition to two blogs, one for the programme[11] and another for the debate on broadband in Peru.[12]

CONCLUSIONS

Social networking services such as Facebook and Twitter are useful as instruments for communication when the message is specific but of interest to a wider audience. In these cases it is possible to construct and share an alternative discourse with numerous followers.

This did not happen for the campaign held in Peru around the National Broadband Plan, because the specificity of the subject required direct contact among the actors, which was finally achieved thanks to internet television and the Código Abierto

---

11 See codigoabiertotv.lamula.pe/

12 See bandaancha.lamula.pe/

software. Online social networking tools will only prove useful as instruments for collective actions if they are sustained by group initiatives. That is to say, social networking tools will not create cooperation and participation scenarios unless there is a pre-existing active community. This was the case in Peru, where the community of ICT and development activists is dispersed and has trouble articulating a common agenda. The most widely used social networks in Peru are related to entertainment, and so are not taken into account by decision makers. The situation is worse because of government institutions' internal policies limiting the use of social network applications and collaborative work because they consider them as a threat to network security and a source of distraction for civil servants.

The impact of this "national laboratory" is connected more with the links and existing communication between the project leader and the members of the committee than with the effectiveness of the tools in providing them with messages and evidence. We also benefited from the reputation the La Mula portal has as an independent medium and from the reputation of DIRSI and IEP, especially among the expert members of the committee.

The process of influencing policy is sustained by the existing trust among participating actors. While we do not recommend employing strategies based exclusively on the use of social networking tools, they can effectively accompany and amplify advocacy activities in formal decision making processes and arenas, such as meetings, seminars and formal correspondence and communication.

REFERENCES

Abdala, M y P. Spiller. 1999. *Instituciones, Contratos y Regulación en Argentina*. Buenos Aires: Temas Grupo Editorial.

Barrantes, R. y A. Agüero. 2010a. *Desarrollo de la Banda Ancha en la Región Andina – Estudio Comparativo de Bolivia, Colombia, Ecuador y Perú*. Lima: DIRSI.

Barrantes, R. y A. Agüero. 2010b. *Estudio sobre la Banda Ancha en el Perú*. Lima: DIRSI.

Barrantes, R. y R. Pérez 2006. "Regulación e Inversión en Telecomunicaciones: el Caso Peruano". *Wdr Dialogue Theme 3rd cycle*. Discussion Paper.

Bossio, J. 2010a. *Entorno Regulatorio de las Telecomunicaciones: Perú 2007 – 2009*. Lima: DIRSI.

Bossio, J. 2010b. "Redes Dorsales de Banda Ancha en América Latina". Proyecto Impacto 2.0. Lima: IEP.

CEPAL. 2010. "La Banda Ancha es Clave en el Círculo Virtuoso del Desarrollo". En *Notas de la CEPAL* 64, abril 2010.

Crewe, Emma y John Young. 2002. "Bridging Research and Policy: Context, Evidence and Links". Londres: ODI.

Jordan, V., H. Galperin y W. Peres. 2010. *Acelerando la Revolución Digital: Banda Ancha para América Latina y el Caribe*. CEPAL-DIRSI.

ONLINE
PUBLIC
CONSULTATIONS

4. INTRODUCTION

Bruce Girard

One way governments can improve their policy proposals is by submitting them to the test of public opinion. Public consultations involve soliciting public and stakeholder input into the policymaking process. Through consultations, policymakers can involve expertise and alternative perspectives in the discussion, or identify opposing interests and invite ideas for how they might be balanced. Consultations can be formal or informal, they can be limited to a handful of key stakeholders, or invite comments from the general public, and they can take place in a single moment or as part of ongoing deliberation. Whatever form they take, the key objectives include to improve the quality of information available to decision-makers, to give citizens and stakeholders a role in discussing policy options and, ultimately, to contribute to better policy.

Traditional consultation processes are conducted during meetings or by inviting the submission of briefs or opinions. Meetings have the advantage of permitting dialogue between and among stakeholders and government, while on the downside they impose severe physical and time constraints –face-to-face dialogue requires everyone to be at the same place at the same time. Inviting written interventions, on the other hand, overcomes problems of time and space, but inhibits dialogue.

The section looks at how the interactive possibilities of the internet were employed to support public consultation processes, convened by policymakers and researchers, that overcome the problems of space and time inherent in consultations based on meetings and written interventions, focusing on recent *consultation 2.0* experiences in Brazil and Uruguay. Fabro Steibel, Federico Beltramelli and Eduardo Alonso evaluate the role of institutions and political practitioners in designing such initiatives in two case studies: a Brazilian initiative to draft legislation on internet governance (the Marco Civil Regulatório or MCR), and an Uruguayan public consultation on digital television broadcasting. In their analysis the authors seek to:

1. formulate hypotheses on what contextual elements favour the launch of online consultations;
2. evaluate how deliberative rules and technology overlap; and
3. map good practices regarding the mix of different web 2.0 technologies for designing online deliberation experiences for drafting legislation and policy.

While the case studies point to the value of involving various stakeholders in public consultations, the evidence indicates that governmental commitment is essential. The Brazilian initiative was led by the Ministry of Justice with the active involvement of the Ministry of Culture and the *Centro de Tecnologia e Sociedade*, a civil society think tank. While the participation of the think tank brought a number of advantages, the consultation was convened and led by the government and the result –draft legislation for governing the internet– was an official document.

This contrasts with Uruguay where the Ministry of Industry, Energy and Mining (MIEM) proposed the virtual public hearing, but then progressively withdrew its support, first declining to convene it, then organising a formal but parallel *public notice-and-comment process*, and finally excluding the results of the consultation from the formal process.

The report compares the differences and similarities of the two consultations, identifies some lessons learned, and points to areas requiring further research. The authors suggest that, despite the pioneering nature of the projects and their very different contexts, both experiences had to deal with similar challenges in mixing policy making, technology and society. Among the key lessons learned are:

1. Online public consultations require openness. Governments and bureaucracies must be open to consulting with citizens on topics of general public interest or public consultations, online or otherwise, will not be successful. For online consultations they must also be willing to use unfamiliar tools and, more importantly, be willing to engage in unfamiliar practices whose very strength lies in their transparency and accessibility. These challenges can require changes in the institutional cultures of governmental institutions more comfortable with announcing decisions than asking for advice.

2. Government institutions matter, a lot. In addition to being open to the idea, successful online consultations require the active support of the sponsoring government institution. Stakeholders and citizens will only engage with the process if they believe the sponsoring institution is taking it seriously and they will be listened to.

3. Researchers and think tanks can play various roles in online consultations. In the cases studied these included designing the consultations, deciding what technologies to incorporate, moderating, providing context and presenting issues and options, and facilitating contact with civil society initiatives.

4. As with any policy consultation, the topic being discussed matters. If people perceive their interests are at stake, they will be more likely to participate. However, online consultations may have their own bias built-in and part of the success of Brazil's consultation can be partially explained by the fact that its topic, internet governance, was perceived as important by "cyberactivists", a community particularly qualified and accustomed to online deliberation.

5. POLICY, RESEARCH AND ONLINE PUBLIC CONSULTATIONS IN BRAZIL AND URUGUAY

Eduardo Alonso, Federico Beltramelli and Fabro Steibel

During 2009 and 2010, Brazil held a public consultation seeking to draft legislation on internet governance. In 2011, in Uruguay, a public consultation was convened to seek input from citizens and stakeholders on the country's policy for digital broadcast television. In the case of Brazil the initiative was led by the Ministry of Justice, working with the Ministry of Culture and the Centro de Tecnologia e Sociedade (Centre for Technology and Society–a civil society think tank). In Uruguay the consultation was initiated by the telecommunications department of the Ministry of Industry, Energy and Mining in cooperation with Fundación Comunica and a group of independent academics, but was quickly transformed when changes within the Ministry left the consultation with no formal connection with the government.

The two consultations were different in many ways. They differed considerably in terms of scale, for example. The Brazilian consultation was held over a total of three months, divided into two separate periods of 45 days each, and attracted over 2,000 contributions and significant media coverage. By contrast, the Uruguayan consultation lasted only 21 days, drew relatively few comments was given very little in-depth media coverage. They also took place in significantly different political and social contexts, for example Brazil has a decentralised federal system of government, while Uruguay's is highly centralised.

What they had in common, however, was that they were online public consultations: understood here as internet-based systems used to support a government request for public input on a particular policy initiative and that facilitate multi-directional communication about the policy between and among government, citizens, and other stakeholders.

This paper analyses the two cases, with a focus on comparing the answers to the two questions guiding the research: (i) what similar impacts did the two experiences achieve, and (ii) what were the common challenges faced by the sponsors of both initiatives?

The paper begins with a brief overview of traditional public consultation tools, followed by the two case studies and finally we present some tentative conclusions and lessons learned.

CONSULTATION TOOLS

Public consultations are one of the key tools available to governments to make the drafting of legislation and policies more transparent, effective and efficient. Consultations are useful in improving the quality of public policies if they increase the quantity and improve the quality of information available to decision makers. Through consultation, policy makers can bring alternative viewpoints and expert knowledge into the discussion, and can also identify conflicting interests and solicit advice on how to balance them.

Consultations imply the active search for contributions from different stakeholders. They can be conducted in different

BOX 1 - Traditional policy consultation tools

A background document produced by the OECD in 2006 describes five types of public consultation:

1. Informal consultation includes "all forms of discretionary, *ad hoc*, and unstandardised contacts" between policy makers and stakeholders, for example informal meetings, letters and telephone conversations. While this type of consultation can be flexible, fast and inexpensive, it lacks transparency and accountability.

2. Circulation of policy proposals for public comment is a consultation process that involves circulating concrete proposals in a more systematic and structured way than with informal consultations. Participation is usually limited to key recognised stakeholders to the exclusion of less-organised groups and the public at large.

3. Public notice-and-comment is a more structured, formal and inclusive consultation than circulation of policy proposals for public comment in that it involves the preparation and distribution of background information, including for example draft legislation, discussion papers about the problem being addressed, policy objectives, impact assessments and alternative solutions, as well as a request for written comment and input.

4. Public hearings are meetings at which interested parties and groups can comment in person. They are usually attached to a public notice-and-comment process and seek to make it even more accessible and even to enable some form of dialogue between and among policymakers, stakeholders and interested members of the public. Nevertheless, the OECD notes two limitations to public hearings: they are likely to be one-off events which may be inaccessible to some and thus require significant coordination, planning and resources to ensure access, and "the simultaneous presence of many groups and individuals with widely differing views can render a discussion of particularly complex or emotional issues impossible, limiting the ability of this strategy to generate empirical information."

5. Advisory bodies can be *ad hoc* or permanent and may be established to provide technical advice or to negotiate interests. While there are many different types of bodies, they have two common features: they have a specific mandate (to provide expertise or seek consensus) and they include people from outside government.

ways, from telephone conversations with representatives of key interest groups, to structured public meetings aimed at involving wider sectors of the public. The OECD, for example, describes five traditional tools for policy consultation (see Box 1).

These different tools meet different objectives and could be used at different points during the policy-making process. Two of them –public notice-and-comment and public hearings– are designed to make public policy making accessible to a non-specialist, wider public, and are therefore particularly suited for policies on issues that will have a significant impact on society.

In practice, public hearings are almost always attached to a public notice-and-comment process. The online consultations presented in this chapter essentially combine these two tools, thus allowing for dialogue among policy makers, stakeholder groups and members of the general public while avoiding many of the limitations of traditional consultations.

While the internet can be used, and is being used, in all of these types of consultation, the possibilities for interaction and collaboration offered by web 2.0 tools and applications could be especially useful for hosting public hearings, since they reduce costs while increasing opportunities for effective participation and eliminating some of the constraints of face-to-face meetings. Of equal importance is the fact that in online consultations, just as in traditional public notice-and-comment processes, a significant effort must be made to provide the public with background information that explains the objectives of the policies in question, identifies alternative solutions, and generally equips interested individuals and organisations with enough knowledge to understand the implications of the policies being discussed.

Based on the five categories of public consultation described in Box 1, we could conclude that the online consultations in both Brazil and Uruguay were similar to traditional public hearings. They were formal consultations, open to the general public, and were conducted early in the policy drafting process in order to contribute to the definition of positions and options. The distribution of background information and description of alternative solutions made them accessible to non-specialists. However, unlike traditional public hearings, the consultations assessed here were conducted online, thus freeing them from the physical and time constraints of conventional hearings.

Another feature shared by the Uruguayan and Brazilian cases is that both were processes initiated by governments seeking the involvement of civil society in public policy deliberation. This analytical categorisation should, in turn, be assessed in relation to the institutional and political framework in each case. In Uruguay, the process was initiated as a government proposal for a virtual public hearing. But this strategy rapidly deteriorated, as the state institution responsible (the telecommunications division of the Ministry of Industry, Energy and Mines) withdrew from its role as convener of the consultation, which created confusion among the target audience as to who was convening the process and for what purpose. By contrast, in Brazil, the continued support of government institutions led to much more coherent results. Thus, although both initiatives were launched on the basis of the same methodology, the outcomes were largely conditioned by the respective institutional and political contexts.

BRAZIL: INSTITUTIONS MATTER

Introduction

In the case of Brazil, research focused on the impact of web 2.0 technologies on the design of deliberative consultations on public policy. More specifically, it evaluated the impact of these technologies on how policy makers and citizens negotiate opportunities for deliberation for the drafting of legislation. As a case study we evaluated the *Marco Civil Regulatório* (MCR) project, an initiative sponsored by the Brazilian government with the main objective of developing draft legislation on internet governance following two cycles of public consultation conducted in 2009 and 2010 with the aid of web 2.0 technologies.

Generally speaking, the MCR project could be considered enormously successful. Defining what "success" means in terms of deliberative practices would require defining normative standards by which participation is evaluated, which is far from a settled matter. Nonetheless, considering that the MCR project was the first of its kind in Brazil, that around 2,000 contributions from the general public were received by the website during the consultation period, that later projects refer to it as a key reference point, and most importantly, that the project succeeded in translating the concerns received online into draft legislation to be sent to Congress, we can argue that the MCR project was indeed enormously successful.

The government's decision to conduct a public consultation to make informed decisions was nothing new. In fact, public consultations are regulated in specific legislation (D4176/2000) in Brazil. What made the MCR project so innovative was not the government's decision to run a public consultation on how to regulate the internet, but rather the decision to conduct it with the aid of the internet itself. Expanding the locus of debate from physical spaces (such as meeting rooms in the capital city of Brasilia) to an open and public URL, capable of hosting a policy debate online, is something that had never been tried before, according to the sources we interviewed.

Our interviewees recalled isolated cases where online technology had been used by the government to consult experts or average citizens, as well cases in which the government had considered conducting public debates online. Nevertheless, the MCR project is perceived as the pioneering experience of its kind, something so important that that the interviewees describe it as an event that "upgraded" the way public consultations are conducted in the country. If we consider that since the MCR project ended, five similar projects have begun, this "upgrade" hypothesis might actually be accurate.

Main conclusion: Institutions matter

According to our research, when it comes to the importance of technology for policy consultation processes, institutions matter a great deal. This supports Blumler and Coleman's (2009) argument that "for democratic participation to have a meaningful impact upon political outcomes there is a need for inclusive and accountable institutions that can provide a space for consequential interaction between citizens and their elected representatives." Our findings suggest that web 2.0 technologies represent a very positive scenario as support tools for future policy-making efforts. However, without institutions backing, designing and moderating the use of web 2.0 technologies for this purpose, technology itself will only have a very limited scope for making real changes to existing legislation.

A central argument of this research is that without the direct support and commitment of government institutions (in this case, the Ministry of Justice and the Ministry of Culture), as well as the support provided by research institutions or think tank (in this case, the Centro de Tecnologia e Sociedade or Centre for Technology and Society at the Getúlio Vargas Foundation), the contributions made by the general public through web 2.0 tools would not have resulted in policy change. This is in line with Blumler and Coleman's (2009) argument that top-down policy-making initiatives have greater chances of achieving real policy change than bottom-up initiatives do. In this regard, although we maintain that people do matter as well, our core argument is that understanding how online policy debate influences what governments do requires understanding the key role of institutions in sponsoring and moderating these policy debate forums.

Overview

This chapter is divided in three sections. The first section discusses how government institutions, technology and people interact to create a successful and stimulating online policy debate forum. It suggests as hypotheses four contextual elements needed to start an online policy consultation forum, namely:

1. A government institution with a real interest in direct public participation
2. An active online community with a strong interest in the topic under discussion
3. An active research institution or think tank willing to bring its own expertise and influence to the project
4. A web 2.0 interface capable of engaging policy makers and citizens in a coherent narrative structure for deliberation.

These hypotheses are speculative, and further research is required to support them. Nonetheless, considering the novelty of the field of research and the quick pace of technological change, we argue that identifying fundamental issues related to online policy debate forums is key to this stage of research.

The second and third sections continue the evaluation of how technology and deliberation interact in online consultation projects, focusing on how policy makers decide what issues to submit to deliberation and how technology will be used to mediate deliberation. From different perspectives, both sections focus on five key decisions that policy makers have to make during the early stages of the policy-making process, namely:

- What policy issues should be open or closed to public deliberation
- What technologies to use or not use to mediate the debate
- How to frame the discussion by preparing and disseminating background documents, policy options, impact studies, and similar documents
- How and when to moderate contributions
- How to translate contributions into a properly formatted legal policy document.

Methodology

The data used in this research came from in-depth interviews conducted with public servants, academics and web designers responsible for planning and executing the MCR project. Interviewees were selected based on a two-round sampling procedure. We first identified potential contacts at the main institutions sponsoring the initiative. After two preliminary rounds of interviews with members of each of these institutions, a second list of names was compiled, including public servants at the Ministry of Culture (who engaged in the project later and were responsible for programming the project website), two public servants from the Ministry of Justice (who coordinated the overall project), and three contributors from the Centre for Technology and Society (the civil society research institution that co-authored the project with the Ministry of Justice).[1] All interviews were semi-structured in-depth expert interviews, and were analysed based on a mixed-method approach to qualitative data analysis.

Contextual elements of the MCR project

The MCR project was a joint initiative of the Ministry of Justice (the project's initiator)[2] and the Centre for Technology and Society (CTS, hosted by the Getúlio Vargas Foundation, a think tank based in Rio de Janeiro). Apart from these two organisations, the project also received direct support from the Ministry of Culture, indirect assistance from other governmental bodies (such as the Ministry of Foreign Affairs), and ad hoc contributions from civil society organisations and a number of internet rights activists. As such, the MCR project

---

1 From the Ministry of Justice, Guilherme Almeida and Paulo Rená; from the "Centro de Tecnologia e Sociedade", Carlos Affonso Pereira de Souza, Pedro Augusto Ferreira Francisco and Marília Maciel; from the Ministry of Culture, José Almeida Júnior.

2 More specifically, the Ministry of Justice's Office of Legislative Affairs.

was a government initiative which, with the aid of an important think thank and of civil society, established itself as a one-of-a-kind online policy debate forum. As the CTS describes the initiative:

> [The MCR was an event where] NGOs, universities, internet service providers, [...] private companies, law firms, law enforcement agencies, individuals, Brazilian embassies all over the world, and many other participants joined in an online public hearing. The participation of various stakeholder groups promoted a diversity of opinions and provided access to high-quality information and expert advice, all of which helped the government to draft a balanced bill.

The general objective of the MCR project was to draft a bill for an internet law to be submitted to a Congressional vote. The bill was intended to establish a set of legal principles and rights to guide future internet legislation in the country, and the entire consultation process was designed to be based on online collaborative practices. The project ran from October 2009 to May 2010, and resulted in an online forum where politicians, academics, artists, NGOs, companies, individuals and other stakeholders with an interest in the topic could post, debate and comment on the possible design of future internet legislation.

The project made use of several web 2.0 tools (mainly a WordPress platform, Twitter, RSS feeds and blogs). It was divided into two rounds of discussion. During the first round, people were invited to comment on a "white paper" with a set of general ideas to broadly orient the draft legislation. During the second round, they were invited to comment on the draft legislation as formatted to be sent to Congress. As the interviewees describe the process, the first round tested a set of normative standards, pre-defined by those sponsoring the initiative, that were considered important to include in future legislation, while the second round focused on receiving feedback on the draft itself.

It is important to note that during both consultation periods, participants could comment only on pre-defined topics, said by the interviewees to focus on three areas of discussion: individual and collective rights (i.e., privacy, freedom of speech and access rights), principles related to intermediaries (i.e., net neutrality and civil liability), and governmental directives (i.e., openness, infrastructure and capacity building). Therefore, although the online consultation project was conceived as a collaborative practice – an initiative open to the general public to engage and share their opinions – citizens were basically invited to offer suggestions, but not to decide what topics were open for debate, nor on the actual wording of the final draft legislation.

According to the interviewees, the MCR project began in September 2009, when public servants from the Ministry of Justice invited policy experts from the CTS to design the online platform. Two months later, the website was launched and the first of two six week consultation periods began. The second six week consultation period ended in mid-2010, when the drafting of the bill was completed. During the two periods of consultation, over 2,000 contributions from individual users, governmental and non-governmental entities were received. Policy makers were responsible for gathering the comments and writing the final draft bill, which comprised 25 articles divided into five chapters concerning users' rights and general principles for the regulation of the internet.

Analysing the interviews, we can see that the MCR project was based on three main tenets:

1. It aimed to design a piece of legislation based on solid judicial grounds, a legal text ready to be sent to Congressional hearings.
2. It aimed to create policies capable of securing existing and future individual rights over the internet.
3. It was intended from the start to be based on collaborative practices and public debate enabled by web 2.0 tools.

The interviewees repeatedly referred to the combination of these three tenets as key motivators behind the MCR online consultation initiative.

The main event mentioned by interviewees to justify the emergence of the MCR project was a bill known as the Lei Azeredo or Azeredo Law. This earlier draft legislation focused on regulating crimes over the internet, and was sent to the Chamber of Deputies (lower house of Congress) in 1999 (PL 84/99), and to the Senate in 2003 (PLS 89/03). The Azeredo Law was heavily criticised by cyber activists, think tanks, and particularly by the government of Luiz Inácio (Lula) da Silva (2002-2010), for seeking to legislate internet crimes in a context where civil rights on the internet had still not been defined. In fact, according to the people we interviewed, the alternative project's name, "Marco Civil Regulatório" ("Civil Regulatory Framework") was chosen precisely to clearly express their opposition to discussing criminal codes of conduct prior to securing civil rights and obligations related to internet use.

Analysing how the Azeredo Law was received in different policy communities in Brazil is key to understanding the context in which the MCR project was conceived. If we analyse the main reasons mentioned by the interviewees to explain why the MCR initiative emerged, we can identify four contextual elements that need to be taken into consideration:

1. The engagement of cyber activists around the social movement known as Mega Não ("Mega No")
2. The activities undertaken by the CTS in opposition to the Azeredo Law's legal principles
3. The political agenda of the executive branch, which supported the definition of the internet as a social right

A shared understanding amongst policy makers that regulating a collaborative environment like the internet required the use of collaborative practices such as those found in the online world

From the very start, the Azeredo Law drew fierce criticism both inside and outside online discussion forums, but it was primarily after 2009, with the launch of the Mega Não blog by cyberactivist João Caribé, that social opposition to the bill gained a coherent voice. The Mega Não movement fuelled intense activism in blogs, Twitter and other social media that not only attracted even more online activists to the cause, but also received media coverage from niche national media, motivated protest marches in several Brazilian cities, and was a theme addressed at important internet-related events throughout that year.

The interviewees reported that the Mega Não movement played a key role in the overall success of the MCR project. It was individuals closely associated with the movement who were the first to contribute to the consultation through the comments section, they said. In addition, activists involved in Mega Não helped to publicise the MCR initiative by using their own Twitter hashtags and blog networks to comment on the initiative.

The interviewees also mentioned that, at first, cyberactivists were suspicious that their "bottom-up" movement would be overlooked by the "top-down" initiative they were being invited to join. Nonetheless, most Mega Não supporters gradually started to trust the MCR initiative as a real opportunity to push forward their own policy interests, which in turn attracted even more contributors and publicity for the MCR website.

Another key element mentioned by interviewees was the policy activism of CTS. CTS was already known nationally and internationally for its policy agenda in favour of open source software, Creative Commons licensing, and other issues associated with the links between technology, law and society. CTS was also known for having published two reports criticising the Azeredo Law proposal, which increased its influence on government bodies, academics and cyberactivist networks.

According to interviewees from the Ministry of Justice, the CTS's public policy stances were amongst the main reasons why it was invited to co-author the MCR project. The Ministry of Justice welcomed the participation of the CTS, not only due to its opposition to the Azeredo Law, but also because of their shared ideas on designing online collaborative venues for policy making. For their part, interviewees from the CTS said they welcomed the Ministry of Justice's invitation because they perceived the initiative as an opportunity to push forward their own policy agenda, as well as a promising opportunity to influence politicians to promote policy debates based on collaborative online practices in the future.

Another key element mentioned by interviewees as decisive in launching the MCR project was the government's support. President Lula's speech at the 2009 International Free and Open Source Software Forum[3] is considered the event that triggered the entire initiative. During his speech, the president explicitly opposed the Azeredo Law proposal, and called for an alternative bill that would protect civil rights on the internet. Lula's speech, however, was far from an isolated event; it simply illustrated a broad agenda pushed forward by the incumbent government to understand the internet as a challenge to ways of thinking about social relations and governance.

As we can see, the conditions for designing the MCR were set: the actors were motivated, and the only thing that was missing was the "place" to hold the debate. The government was determined to conduct a public consultation, which is why the Ministry of Justice invited a civil society think tank to co-author the initiative. Civil society was also committed to a public debate, as had been made clear by the active engagement around the Mega Não movement. All that was needed was a place where government and citizens could meet, discuss and deliberate. Web 2.0 tools were used to create that "place".

It should be noted that there had been experiences in the use of the internet in policy making prior to the Lula government.

---

3 10º Fórum Internacional de Software Livre, Porto Alegre, 24-27 March 2009.

As early as 1999 there had been pilot initiatives using IRC chat technology and blogs, for example. Nevertheless, the interviewees reported that after Lula took office in 2002, the use of the internet for policy development expanded considerably. Two internet-related projects implemented by the Ministry of Culture were mentioned as illustrative of this change of direction. The first, known as Pontos de Cultura, involved the allocation of government funding to local cultural centres for the provision of internet access to local communities. The second, CulturaDigital.Br, invited citizens to create and share their blogs and digital identities on a public and open-source WordPress-based platform in order to foster policy deliberation online.

The last contextual element mentioned by the interviewees was the emergence of new ways of linking law, society and technology. Due to the emergence of collaborative and network-based technology, interviewees considered it necessary to re-conceptualise how their institutions understood knowledge production. The CTS, the Ministry of Justice and the Ministry of Culture had pioneered several experiments in previous years investigating alternative governance models based on technology. The CTS, for example, had been influential in supporting the use of Creative Commons licensing; the Ministry of Justice and Ministry of Culture had piloted the portal CulturaDigital.Br, inviting cyberactivists and hackers to share their opinions online. Within this context, the interviewees welcomed the MCR project as an opportunity to try out alternatives to the traditional government-centred, closed-doors process of policy making. As one interviewee put it, the MCR initiative was a "movement of symbiosis between the way you define policy making and the object of policy regulation [...] and it is within this 'happy marriage' between these two elements that we defined what we aimed to achieve."

The early stages of policy consultation

Although the MCR project officially started in late 2009, its origins date back at least 30 years. Public consultations are a common practice in democratic governance, because governments are expected to consult people before making decisions that affect them. In order to consult the public, a government must first design collaborative tools to engage citizens in policy making. In Brazil, regulations were established for public hearings back in the late 1980s, and they are now used as an administrative tool by all branches of government (Soares, 2002). We can also trace back to 1995 the first government institution specifically created to regulate the internet, the Brazilian Internet Steering Committee (CGI.br), which was also given the responsibility for designing new forms of public consultation.[4] We can therefore argue that the Brazilian government has at least 30 years of experience in designing tools for collaborative practices, at least half of it based on some expertise in the use of web tools.

One way to understand how policy discussion forums are affected by web 2.0 tools would be to evaluate, once the public consultations are over, what answers citizens provided to the government and what uses the government made of these contributions. However, this analysis would have to be undertaken during later stages of policy making, and could not be applied in our research. Instead, this section focuses on earlier stages of deliberative processes, specifically evaluating how policy makers decided –before the public was invited to contribute online– what policy questions were open or closed to deliberation, and which technologies were used to mediate the debate.

In the case of the MCR project, understanding which policy issues were open or closed was straightforward: one page of the MCR website was used to list all topics open for discussion (e.g., civil

---

4 CGI www.cgi.br/english

responsibility of internet users, freedom of expression, privacy and net neutrality) and another to list all topics closed to debate (e.g., copyright, data protection and child pornography).

Beyond defining which issues are open or closed for discussion in policy debates (i.e., defining what people will deliberate about), designing rules for policy debates also requires identifying and selecting tools to allow people and institutions to share their opinions with each other (i.e., deciding how people will deliberate). In "offline" policy forums, such as those regularly run by the Congress in public meeting rooms, policy makers have to decide how large the meeting venues need to be, what time and date they will take place, and how those in attendance can effectively share their opinions. In policy forums held online, similar decisions need to be made addressing other issues, such as how people will have access to the forum's website, what coding language the website will be written in, how comments will be displayed online, and how people will post their opinions.

Due to the pioneering nature of online projects like the MCR initiative, we observed that designing rules to decide what people can debate over is a much simpler task than deciding how technology will be used for deliberation.

The interviewees reported that they made decisions on which issues to include based on several background research tools they had at hand: they identified policy issues already under discussion in other spheres of government, selecting topics that would increase the chances of obtaining support inside Congress, or that were likely to increase the project's audience. Based on these analyses (which are the same as those used for "offline" policy consultations), policy makers had plenty of sources of input to strategically decide on what mix of policy issues was likely to increase the overall success of the project.

However, the same cannot be said when we analyse the decisions about how technology should be used for deliberation. As the interviewees repeatedly stressed, the MCR project was a highly experimental and challenging initiative. They reported, for example, that they chose to use WordPress based on the open-source nature of this technology. This decision was also influenced by their personal expertise and experience in running blogs of their own, as well as their awareness of the Ministry of Culture's CulturaDigital.Br initiative (which was later used to host the project website). The decision to create a comments section based on a "paragraph-by-paragraph" layout was inspired by their previous knowledge of The Public Index (a collaborative blog created at New York Law School to discuss Google Books' policies),[5] although they needed to make a number of adjustments before it met their needs. Even decisions on which technology choices to continue or discontinue were made on an ad hoc basis, in response to the feedback received. For example, the overall layout of the comments section received positive feedback, which led to the use of a similar but improved layout for the second phase of consultation. On the other hand, the use of a "thumbs up/thumbs down" voting system was removed shortly after implementation due to the negative feedback received from users.

Governments might opt to run public consultations fully "offline" (i.e., without the use of online tools) or decide to do it "online" (i.e., with the aid of internet tools), but either way, if governments want to hear what citizens have to say, some tools and technologies must be used (i.e. postal mail, public meetings, surveys) to enable the exchange of communication.

If we compare offline and online policy consultations, we can see that decisions made during the early stages of designing policy forums, about what to deliberate on, are similar for both. However, decisions that must be made regarding how the deliberations will be structured and moderated are not so similar.

The experimental and rapidly changing nature of initiatives such

5 thepublicindex.org/introduction (accessed 29 March 2012)

as the MCR project do not mean that the decisions made by policy makers are based on random information gathered through fluctuating processes, but they do challenge the understanding of how well-established policy-making practices (such as mapping competing policy agendas before deciding on what policy agenda to adopt) interact with experimental practices of policy consultation and policy making using web 2.0 tools.

Best practices and discussion

Institutions matter: this was the key lesson that emerged from the MCR initiative. In this case, employing new ICT tools to expand citizen engagement in public policy making would not have been possible without the commitment and support of the Ministry of Justice and the CTS in designing and implementing methodologies for using technology for public consultation. In the executive summary of the 2003 OECD report on e-democracy (Macintosh 2003), Stephen Coleman raises three main lessons learned from the case studies analysed, which are also useful to summarise the lessons learned in the MCR initiative.

The first lesson is that "technology is an enabler not the solution. Integration with traditional, 'offline' tools for access to information, consultation and public participation in policy-making is needed to make the most of ICTs." As we can see in the case of the MCR project, web 2.0 tools facilitated communication between policy makers and citizens, but they did not define the overall project. The interviewees believe, for example, that the impact of the project went beyond the limits of its web presence. They mentioned the number of journalists who requested interviews and who published articles on the topic. They also noted that they used the website to make copies of press clippings accessible online to everyone. Because they posted "everything", including articles critical of the initiative, they feel they gained trust not only from journalists, but from the general public as well.

Twitter is another example of how technology was used to facilitate communication between policy makers and citizens, but did not define the overall project. Twitter was widely used to promote the initiative through "tweets" with URLs for the website home page as well as specific sections of the debate. The interviewees believe that this spurred many blogs, online forums and other "places" to begin hosting their own debates and promoting their own URLs on Twitter.

The use of ICTs also influenced the policy agendas of other stakeholders. Due to the visibility that the MCR project achieved online, even offline interactions between the project leaders and other government institutions were impacted. The interviewees reported that at one point during the consultation period, the Federal Police contacted the Ministry of Justice to express their opposition to a particular policy proposal. The MCR project representatives maintain that the police became aware of the issue though the online consultation, and that prior to the consultation, internet legislation had not been on the police force's agenda. According to its organisers, the MCR initiative motivated the police, and other institutions, to join the debate about Brazil's future internet legislation.

The second lesson mentioned in the OECD report is that "the online provision of information is an essential precondition for engagement, but quantity does not mean quality. Active promotion and competent moderation are key to effective online consultations." As mentioned above, without the intervention of policy makers, the more than 2,000 comments posted online would not have been translated into a properly formatted policy document to be submitted to Congress. In addition, the active moderation by policy makers was described as essential to maintain a certain level of debate. The interviewees reported that no defamatory comments were circulated online during the entire consultation period, but added that they had discussed internally the eventual need to intervene if necessary, as well as the possible need to monitor the site. Another decision made by the interviewees was to avoid sharing their own policy views in the comments section, leaving the debate section open for members of the public to discuss the issues among peers. They believe that this was viewed by users as evidence of the transparency and openness of the project's sponsors.

The third and final lesson mentioned in the OECD report is that "the barriers to greater online citizen engagement in policy-making are cultural, organisational and constitutional not technological. Overcoming these challenges will require greater efforts to raise awareness and capacity both within governments and among citizens." As the interviewees describe it, web 2.0 tools allowed different publics to engage in the consultation process, including some that are usually absent from such practices. For example, they reported with surprise the willingness of cyberactivists and videogame players to discuss the future legislation of the internet. Eventually, the interest of these young people in the MCR initiative motivated policy makers to present the project at Campus Party, a well-known online entertainment event in Brazil.

Web tools also motivated experts not previously involved in the debate to share their ideas. The interviewees commented, for example, on a healthy "online battle" between two experts supporting different proposals to regulate log records kept by internet service providers. The debate started in the comments section, but it became so extensive (in terms of both the length and number of comments) that the sponsors decided to publish it on the main page as a properly formatted text compiling the contributions of each author.

URUGUAY: A CONSULTATION WITHOUT COMMITMENT

In 2010 the government of Uruguay announced that it was preparing draft legislation to streamline and systematise regulations governing the telecommunications sector and the process of technological convergence affecting the media.

The National Telecommunications Department (DINATEL) – a specialised division of the Ministry of Industry, Energy and Mines (MIEM) –launched a timeline of activities that included the creation of a Technical Consultative Committee (CTC). This 30-member committee was made up of representatives of a wide range of civil society and private sector organisations involved in the field, who were brought together to offer opinions and make proposals.

The activities also included a series of conferences with international experts, the organisation of thematic debates and forums, and the creation of a website. Initially, the site was to be used to receive contributions from other stakeholders and to publish reports of the deliberations and conclusions of the CTC, so as to make the process more transparent.

By late 2010 the CTC had drafted a document which compiled the main contributions received. As a consultation process, the CTC was a classic advisory body,[6] which used the internet in an innovative way to increase the transparency of the process and to invite other stakeholders to contribute to the debate (Rodríguez 2011).

Thanks to the success of the CTC's work, there was an explicit willingness, expressed in numerous documents and public statements by MIEM sub-secretary Edgardo Ortuño and the director of DINATEL at the time, Gustavo Gómez, to open up discussion on other issues related to communications policy to more stakeholders and the general public.

Framework and background of the Uruguay Public Consultation Project

Beginning in March 2011, representatives of DINATEL and Fundación Comunica held a series of talks with our research

---

6 See Box 1 on page 89

team on the subject of "virtual" public consultations and the possibility of using them to support DINATEL's work in the drafting of different policies. We agreed to carry out a public consultation that would be planned by our research team, convened by DINATEL, and jointly implemented.

We considered a number of different subjects, including the proposals that had emerged from the CTC for new legislation on audiovisual services, and finally decided to focus on the digital television broadcasting policy that DINATEL was working on at the time and which we considered to be a more manageable issue for a first experience. It was agreed that the consultation would take place between 22 September and 7 October 2011, later extended to 14 October.

In terms of the traditional policy consultation tools outlined at the beginning of this paper, the consultation was originally conceived as a virtual public hearing, with the addition of a few key elements of a public notice-and-comment process.

As well as providing a space for interested individuals and stakeholder groups to make comments on a series of proposals, the process also aimed to enhance the public's capacity to participate effectively, by offering background information (articles, regulatory documents, proposals for alternative solutions). This background information was particularly important for addressing the subject of digital television broadcasting and other similar issues related to telecommunications in Uruguay, where the general public is normally cut off from the debate and unaware of the real impacts of information and communications public policy guidelines in the face of the advent of new technologies. As revealed in a survey we conducted in October 2011 for DINATEL, the public was largely unaware of the debate that was subject of the public consultation. There was also little awareness of the government's plans to table a bill for a new law on audiovisual communications services, despite media coverage on the matter.

	Yes	No
Knowledge of the existence of a debate on the issue	15%	85%
Knowledge of the government's plans to present a new regulatory law	23%	77%

Source: Developed by the authors based on a survey of 1,002 respondents throughout the country in October 2011.

The consultation was to be convened by DINATEL, which would also have the last word regarding the content and general design of the consultative process. In other words, similar to the Brazilian case this was initially planned as a government consultation.

DINATEL, through its director, Gustavo Gómez, actively participated in the design of the consultation, contributing ideas for the design and the proposal in general.

The academic community also played a very active role, providing a number of the articles included on the site to encourage or frame the debate and participation. The citizens would be given a public and horizontal space where they could express themselves, and the government would have a commitment to listen to them.

This situation changed abruptly in early August, when the minister of Industry, Energy and Mines announced that Gustavo Gómez would be removed from his post as the director of DINATEL at the end of October. This was the first of two unexpected actions by the minister, and it meant that although Gómez would continue as nominal director of DINATEL until the end of the consultation, he was forced to reconsider his decision to convene it and even to participate in it.[7] Gómez's

---

[7] The reasons for the removal of Gómez from his post were never clearly explained by the minister, Roberto Kreimerman, who stated that "there have been differences in working methods, but within a climate of great mutual respect." However, neither the consultation nor policies related to digital television appear to have been motives. According to most observers, it was the result of differences over telecommunications policies, an area that also falls under the remit of DINATEL.

decision to adopt a low profile following the announcement of his exit from DINATEL changed the fundamental nature of the initiative, which went from being a government-convened consultation to merely a government-supported consultation.

The second unexpected action by the minister occurred at the end of the first week of the consultation. When a draft version of a presidential decree on regulation of the transition to digital television broadcasting was leaked to the press on 28 September, the minister immediately responded by publishing the draft legislation on the ministry's website and requesting feedback and comments on it.

While this official consultation process was limited,[8] because it asked for comments to be addressed directly to the ministry and no background or contextual information was provided, the fact that it was launched in parallel to the online public consultation, and with no prior communication with the team responsible for it, served as a clear signal that the public consultation was no longer supported by the government. It had become a citizen-led process, an unofficial consultation, without even any guarantee that the government would take its results into account.

Content of the website consultapublica.org.uy

The consultapublica.org.uy website was created to enable the development of an open debate, one that would bring together government authorities, the academic community, the business community and social and political organisations with an interest in the issue of digital television.

It was aimed at fostering informed and inclusive deliberation, and at reaching the widest possible range of public opinion.

---

8 According to the categories outlined previously, the minister's consultation was essentially a "circulation of policy proposals for public comment", with participation "limited to key recognised stakeholders to the exclusion of less-organised groups and the public at large."

The site presented an overview of the main areas of discussion around the potential impact of the introduction of digital television broadcasting on Uruguayan society. It also offered the opinions of influential actors in the political and academic spheres, to allow the public to compare and contrast various opinions and positions regarding the digital television policies best suited to our country.

The information shared on the website was divided into three thematic areas or dimensions. For each dimension, the site offered:

1. A brief introduction to the theme, written by a specialist and expressed in a clear, straightforward manner, so that anyone visiting the site could become better informed about the issues and compare the positions put forward before expressing their own.

2. A "vox populi" style video reflecting different views on the advent of digital television (expectations, knowledge on the subject, general opinions).

3. Academic articles meant to foster debate. These included opinion pieces by different actors involved in the discussions held during 2010, as well as others with an influence on public opinion, in addition to academic reports with varying degrees of depth and detail, adaptable to different potential audiences, with an emphasis on making information accessible to a non-specialist public.

4. Forums for discussion in response to "trigger" questions. It is noteworthy that among the opinions voiced in the discussion forums during the consultation, there were a number of comments that expressed either agreement or disagreement with specific articles.

5. Multiple-choice survey questions.

6. News articles on the subject and links to other websites were provided to direct visitors to other sources of more in-depth information on specific themes.

Visitors were able to comment on all of the articles, news stories and surveys after registering on the site, which fostered exchange and interaction. The forums and articles were specially designed to promote more informed participation, with a certain grasp of the subject matter. To take part in the multiple-choice surveys, visitors did not need to be registered, but could simply click on a response to each question.

The graphic design of the site was aimed at making it user-friendly, straightforward and visually attractive. Accounts linked to the site were created on the social networks Facebook (the groups ConsultaPública and Televisión digital en Uruguay) and Twitter (*@consultapublica*), to allow for wider dissemination of the content of the site and promote discussion in other forums. News stories, excerpts of comments from the site and all new content posted on the site were also posted on these networks.

The thematic dimensions selected were: (i) Institutions: Inclusion and transparency; (ii) Regulation and regulators; (iii) Use of the electromagnetic spectrum.

Political contingency and change in strategy

As we noted earlier, during the implementation of the online public consultation on digital TV between 22 September and 14 October 2011, two events occurred that substantially changed the basic premises of this initiative. The first was the announcement of the imminent removal of Gustavo Gómez from his post as director of DINATEL by the MIEM minister, Roberto Kreimerman. The second was the leak, on 28 September, of an important draft decree that directly concerned the central theme of the online consultation – a leak that also gave rise to the parallel consultation, limited but official, conducted by the ministry itself.

The separation of Gómez from his post affected the initiative in the following ways:

1. Before it was even launched, the public consultation lost the support of the main stakeholder behind it.

2. The dissemination of the public consultation would no longer involve the direct participation of Gustavo Gómez or DINATEL.

3. Without an official counterpart in the government, the initiative would be an unofficial consultation, without formal government support.

While we considered taking advantage of a the fact that Gómez would continue to exercise the position of director of DINATEL during the consultation, his imminent departure would not have passed for formal support. It may also have been possible to gain the endorsement of some other government official, but without MIEM's official support the consultation would be unable to be part of a formal process for public policy making. It was at this point that we decided to conduct an indirect public consultation, one that was not formally convened by the government.

The consultation was thus convened by Fundación Comunica, and its dissemination was limited to the efforts the organisation was able to make with the support of the university researchers responsible for the project, who made contact with different networks in the field of communications, academic entities such as the School of Communications Sciences at the University of the Republic and the Uruguayan Association of Political Science, and organisations like the Coalition for Democratic Communication and the Association of Producers and Filmmakers (ASOPROD), in addition to a number of news stories in the traditional media.

The leak of the draft decree helped raise the visibility of the subject matter of the consultation, which served to revive the issue and the consultation's website, where we quickly published the draft decree and established a special forum for discussion of it. It also sparked an increase in participation and contributed to one of our most important objectives: facilitating and interaction between the government's proposal, academic input, political opinions and political party stances, all in open view of the public. However, the dialogue was never direct nor promoted by state institutions, but was instead guided by the interests of the media agenda and systematised through the website's tools: the surveys, discussion forums and articles.

Two consultations and two models

While the leak of the draft decree revived interest in the subject, the minister's decision to publish the decree and launch a parallel consultation to this research team's public consultation marked a definitive end to the connection between our team and the ministry.[9] The result was a set of "parallel consultations", two processes taking place simultaneously. One was a consultation that sought to reach and engage the general public, while the other was aimed at incorporating specific demands from stakeholders directly involved in the audio-visual industry.

The MIEM's official consultation drew contributions from two private citizens and ten institutions: the MELISA Network (an Ibero-American network aimed at increasing the accessibility of digital television to reduce the digital divide), the School of Communications Sciences of the University of the Republic, the Coalition for Democratic Communication, the Chamber of Uruguayan Pay TV operators, a private television station, three cable television companies, the telecoms company Claro

---

9 The official consultation was limited to the publication of the draft decree and an invitation for the submission of comments. "The aim of the consultation is to provide a space for the general public to express opinions and make proposals on the draft decree on open terrestrial digital television (…). For this purpose, the text of the draft will be available for the next 7 days on the website of the MIEM. Comments, proposals and suggestions can be sent by electronic mail (…); or through a signed letter (…). The comments received will be published on the MIEM and DINATEL website once the consultation period has ended." www.presidencia.gub.uy/wps/wcm/connect/presidencia/portalpresidencia/comunicacion/comunicacionnoticias/miem-abre-consulta-publica-decreto-television-digital-terrestre-abierta-tvd

(Telcom), the Uruguayan chapter of the World Association of Community Radio Broadcasters (AMARC), and the National Association of Uruguayan Broadcasters.[10] Due to the format of this consultation, the proposals put forward were essentially reactions to the draft decree, or quite often simply a reiteration of the positions stated by certain stakeholders in the framework of the CTC, or a defence of corporate interests in the face of a possible restructuring of the ecosystem of audiovisual communications services in Uruguay.

On the other hand, in our consultation the participation of industry actors and representatives of state institutions was nil and many of the organisations that make up the Coalition for Democratic Communication, which had been very active throughout the formal process led by DINATEL during 2010 in the framework of the CTC, chose not to participate in our consultation, even though they were expressly convened.

Comparatively speaking, the format chosen by the MIEM was a bureaucratic and formal exercise in seeking the input of key stakeholders, while our consultation was meant to foster participation by citizens, as well as professional associations, the private sector and political parties. While the methodology used for the MIEM consultation did not offer any possibility for dialogue with the ministry or among the participants, and simply provided email and regular mailing addresses, the general strategy of the consultapublica.org.uy site was to encourage the highest possible degree of horizontal exchange and the inclusion of citizens' views in the policy-making process.

As for the input gathered through consultapublica.org.uy, the ministry did not ask for it and no reference is made to it in the report on the official consultation, although the minister had stated unofficially that it would be taken into account.

---

10 The contributions were published at: www.miem.gub.uy/gxpfiles/miem/content/video/source0000000059/VID0000050000001801.pdf www.miem.gub.uy/gxpfiles/miem/content/video/sourceC000000059/VID0000050000001802.pdf

The two consultations had different objectives and therefore had very different results. We believe our initiative was much more aligned with a pluralistic participatory approach, with emphasis placed on developing a public space for the deliberation of reasoning and arguments, while the MIEM initiative was a traditional consultation aimed at drawing input from specific interest groups. As such, it attracted participation from traditional corporate and private stakeholders, aimed at directly influencing the public policy in question and the policy makers responsible for it. From this perspective, the MIEM consultation was much more successful in its policy impact than the civil society consultation.

The changes and their impact

The fact that the Uruguayan public was presented with two simultaneous "consultations" reflects a certain rigidity and inertia in the country's political routines, but also demonstrates the Uruguayan state's shortcomings in terms of pubic management of the legal framework of public affairs. The lack of coordination among agencies, ministries and the president's office attests to efforts undertaken by government leaders as opposed to precise practices or protocols to promote discussion of public policies that address common goods and universal rights.

Policy making in Uruguay follows a rigidly conventional and institutionalised course. As the result of a heavily party-centric model, policy tends be formulated incrementally with input limited to that of political parties, and in some cases, state or private sector organisations or companies.

An analysis of the events allows us to infer some of these problem areas and at the same time observe efforts to introduce change. The initial enthusiasm for consultation under Gustavo Goméz's directorship is an example of this. However, the political system was not sufficiently robust to follow through with this innovative practice, and resorted to a centralism anchored in political parties as the principal means of defining of public policies.

Policy making remains the preserve of parliamentarians, leading to a situation in which debates are often little more than "mock" debates due to their complexity, with no citizen participation and often without the involvement of the academic community in the formulation of regulatory and legal frameworks and no direct channels for empirical evidence and specialist knowledge to reach policy makers.

The public consultation carried out in Uruguay also demonstrated:

- The lack of legal protocols for the realisation of direct government-led public consultations with citizen participation for the development of laws and regulations, with the exception of the referendum mechanism.

- The existence of strong competition among Uruguayan state institutions in the telecommunications area, regarding which is the regulatory authority and which is responsible for policy design, in addition to some entities that act simultaneously as regulators and commercial operators, as in the case of the state-owned telecoms company ANTEL.

- The designation of political appointees to leadership positions in these agencies adds to the weakness of their management, as these political appointments tend to be made on the basis of a distribution of posts among internal sectors of the political parties in power.

- The presidential system of government, with a particularly strong role played by the executive branch, often makes it difficult for agencies like DINATEL and the Uruguayan telecoms regulator, URSEC, to perform their duties independently, especially since the institutional structure places them in a position of direct dependency on the particular administration in power.

- The lack of a unified legal framework for services in the audiovisual communications and telecommunications sectors is a source of confusion. Institutional jurisdictions are complicated due to the complexity of overlapping, redundant and often limited legal structures.

• Regulation through presidential decree creates a situation with considerable discretionary and exclusive power on the part of the executive branch.

TENTATIVE CONCLUSIONS

Beyond the differences and similarities between the two case studies, a number of tentative conclusions can be drawn as lessons learned from the experiences.

1. For a public consultation to be successful, the state must be willing and able to sponsor it, ensuring from the beginning that sufficient financial and human resources are available. Additionally, sponsoring government institutions must make a commitment to taking the results of the consultation into account.

The two public consultation experiences analysed here demonstrate that government institutions matter, and to a great extent. Government support (or the lack of it) proved to be a fundamental factor in the overall success of each initiative. In the case of Brazil, the support of the Ministry of Justice and Ministry of Culture was decisive in the planning, promotion and implementation of the consultation. In Uruguay, the lack of consistent support from DINATEL and the MIEM severely compromised the project's activities.

However, while online consultations may serve as an important forum for the exercise of democracy, neither the issues defined nor the solutions proposed through public consultations have the power of actual legislation. In Brazil, the online consultation resulted in the drafting of a bill to be sent to Congress, but more than a year later, it has still not been voted into law. In Uruguay, on the other hand, the input received from the "unofficial" public consultation was ignored by the ministry.

It may be true that extra-governmental participation (by citizens, stakeholder groups, etc.) in the policy-making process is wider when consultations are conducted online, instead of behind closed doors, because of greater visibility, transparency and collaboration. Nevertheless, online forums still largely depend on the legislative and executive powers to ensure their significance and impact.

It should be noted that Brazil has specific legislation regulating public consultations, and, as a result of the MCR experience, the regulation of online consultations have been included in that legislation. In Uruguay, however, there is no legislation that regulates public consultations.

2. Another area in which government participation proved to be important was in publicising the initiative.

In Brazil, the policy makers involved participated in the largest possible number of conferences and events to promote the project. They also recognised the importance of media coverage, and used their Twitter accounts and websites to increase the exposure of the media coverage received.

In Uruguay, on the other hand, dissemination was limited almost entirely to academic networks, a handful of news articles, and very slight coverage in the mass media. The Uruguayan experience clearly demonstrated the importance of the political resources of the state as the sponsor of a consultation process (as well as the economic and administrative resources it can provide), regardless of the format chosen.

3. Thirdly, we could stress the importance of the role of academic institutions.

In the case of Brazil, the support of the CTS was decisive for choosing which platform to use, deciding how comments would be moderated, and collaborating with government institutions in the final drafting the bill. The participation of the CTS, an organisation with recognised experience on the issue, also enhanced the legitimacy of the consultation and demonstrated that the government took extra-governmental participation seriously.

In the case of Uruguay, a team of researchers from the University of the Republic were commissioned by a civil society organisation to design and operate the web platform and to select the materials considered necessary to provide background information to participants in the consultation. In both cases, the participation of the academic community ensured that academic research played a key role in deliberations.

4. Another challenge lies in attracting the participation of stakeholder groups in online consultations.

In Uruguay, policy making is carried out within traditional and institutionalised spaces, under considerable party-centred and/ or stakeholder influence. This meant that, given the possibility of participating in an open online public consultation and/or sending comments directly to the ministry, most stakeholder groups, from both the private sector and civil society, opted for more traditional (and more direct) channels.

In Brazil, the policy makers were surprised by how sectors of the public who normally ignore policy making initiatives participated in the debate. At the same time, traditional stakeholders, especially from the private sector, were reticent to share their contributions online, presumably preferring the more direct, and less public, channels. Numerous companies, for example, attempted to send their input by email or letter instead of using the website's public forums. The consultation insisted on transparency, however, and only accepted letters and emails if their authors agreed to allow them to be published on the website.

5. Finally, as with any policy consultation, the topic being discussed matters.

If people perceive their interests are at stake, they will be more likely to participate. Moreover, precisely because there are private or institutional interests at stake, democratic policy making processes should implement consultations with stakeholders to ensure that all of them are considered and to seek consensus among conflicting interests.

However, online consultations have a built-in bias. For example, part of the success of the Brazilian consultation may be explained by the fact that its topic, internet governance, was perceived as important by "cyberactivists", a community particularly qualified and accustomed to online deliberation. In fact, similar consultations carried out after the MCR initiative – one on personal data protection and another on intellectual property – did not inspire the same degree of interest in the public.

REFERENCES

Blumler, J. G. y S. Coleman. 2009. *The Internet and Democratic Citizenship:* Theory, Practice and Policy (p. ix, 220 p.). Cambridge: Cambridge University Press.

D4176. 2002. *Decreto no 4.176, de 28 de Março de 2002.* Presidência da República, Casa Civil, Subchefia para Assuntos Jurídicos. Brasilia. www.planalto.gov.br/ccivil_03/decreto/2002/D4176.htm

Freedman, Des. 2008. *The Politics of Media Policy.* Cambridge: Polity Press.

Macintosh, Ann. 2003. *Promise and Problems of E-Democracy: Challenges of Online Citizen Engagement.* Paris: OECD www.oecd.org/dataoecd/9/11/35176328.pdf

PL 84/99. 1999. *Projeto de Lei. Dispõe sobre os crimes cometidos na área de informática, suas penalidades e dá outras providências.* Brasilia: Cámara dos Deputados. www.camara.gov.br/proposicoesWeb/fichadetramitacao?idProposicao=15028

PLC 89/03. 2003. *Projeto de Lei. Dispõe sobre os crimes cometidos na área de informática, e suas penalidades, dispondo que o acesso de terceiros, não autorizados pelos respectivos interessados, a informações privadas mantidas em redes de computadores, dependerá de prévia autorização judicial.* Brasilia: Senado Federal. www.senado.gov.br/atividade/materia/detalhes.asp?p_cod_mate=63967

Rodríguez, Lourdes. 2011. *Hacia una Ley de Servicios de Comunicación Audiovisual: Relatoría del Proceso de Participación y Consulta.* Montevideo: Friedrich Ebert Stiftung.

Soares , E. 2002. "A Audiência Pública no Processo Administrativo". *Revista do Ministério Público do Trabalho*, v. 12, n. 24, p. 22-49, 2002.

EXPLORATIONS

6. INTRODUCTION

Bruce Girard

While campaigns and public consultations were the areas where our research had the most complete results, the many small projects conducted under the Impact 2.0 umbrella also analysed other areas, prepared materials to support further experimentation, learned lessons and in some cases simply stumbled upon unexpected emerging trends and uses of online social networking services for linking research and policy.

For example, some projects attempted to bring researchers, policymakers and other stakeholders together in online spaces with the more-or-less explicit objective of getting them to know each other better and to build confidence. Others examined whether various stakeholders are ready to use the new tools and applications and attempted to identify the barriers to their use in terms of access, capacity, interest and policy. Another of the project's outputs was the *Impact 2.0 iGuide*, a wiki-based manual designed to help researchers use social networking tools (i) to better understand the policy context; (ii) to encourage discussion, debate and collaboration based on their research findings; and (iii) to develop and maintain relations with policy makers and other stakeholders.

This section brings together these preliminary experiences as short case studies, research reports and articles that identify areas for future research.

7. FOUR EXPERIENCES OF COMMUNICATION, COLLABORATION AND TRUST BUILDING

Estela Acosta y Lara

This section provides an overview of four projects supported by Impact 2.0 that tested the use of social web applications for (i) communicating research findings to non-academic audiences, including policy makers; (ii) collaboration between researchers and policy makers in the design of evidence-based policy proposals; and (iii) strengthening relations between researchers, decision makers and other stakeholders with an interest in a given public policy.

New ICTs in general and social web tools in particular can:

Expand the dissemination of messages, to reach a larger and more diverse audience and thus increase the potential recipients of the information being communicated.

- Lower the costs of production and presentation of information in different formats –both traditional and innovative– adapted to the audience to be reached.
- Foster collaborative work in online arenas between different

actors involved in the design of public policies, in order to incorporate contributions based on academic research evidence.

- Establish and strengthen relations through social networks.
- Each of the projects presented in this section sought to incorporate web technologies to improve communication and increase policy impact. Two of the projects evaluated seem to indicate that web 2.0 environments are conducive to creating spaces for deliberation and consensus building. However, they also confronted challenges. Consistent with similar studies carried out in other regions,[1] it was found that academic researchers share a series of reservations about the use of social networks and other social web tools, which range from issues of security around the publication of their work products, to a lack of knowledge of the potential capacity of these tools, to practical difficulties such as the lack of time and incentives to assess the extremely numerous and ever-changing web 2.0 applications available.

The evaluations of these experiences highlight the importance of the legitimacy and credibility of the research centres sponsoring the initiative when it comes to successfully eliciting collaboration (as in the case, for example, of the Costadigital project). They also underscore the importance of establishing clear and well-defined objectives in terms of the desired outcome of collaborative work (for instance, executive summaries on specific health policies, as in the case of EVIPNet), and of the tools selected to create spaces for this collaboration (the lack of knowledge and practical experience in using a wiki application was one of the main obstacles faced by the CLAEH project).

---

1 Procter et al. 2010 "Adoption and use of Web 2.0 in scholarly communications". In Phil.Trans. R. Soc. A 368, 4039–4056. Brown C. 2011 "Are southern academics virtually connected? A review of the adoption of web 2.0 tools for research collaboration by development researchers in the South". GDNet.

As noted in the conclusions of a recent literature review, "There are a number of activities that can facilitate the process of incorporating knowledge in policy: communication, translation, interaction and exchange, using social influence and intermediaries."[2] The projects presented here demonstrate that the internet and web 2.0 have the capacity to facilitate all of these activities; all that is needed is further research.

EVIPNET-AMERICAS ONLINE COLLABORATIVE SPACE

Due to the growing interest in incorporating scientific evidence into health policy decision-making processes, networks of researchers and decision makers in different regions of the world have come together in recent years in order to promote the use of evidence in the design and implementation of health policies. One of these initiatives, promoted by the World Health Organization (WHO), is EVIPNet (EVidence-Informed Policy Network), a global network that "promotes partnerships at the country level between policy-makers, researchers and civil society in order to facilitate both policy development and policy implementation through the use of the best scientific evidence available."[3] Coordinated in the Americas region by the Pan American Health Organization (PAHO), the EVIPNet Secretariat has been supporting workshops in participating countries that bring together various actors to prepare policy briefs on national health issues. Among the many difficulties of drafting these briefs are the logistical challenges involved in scheduling work sessions with busy people who live in different parts of the country.

Information and communication technologies (ICT) make it possible to overcome geographic and temporal gaps by creating

2 Jones, Harry. 2009 "Policy-making as discourse: a review of recent knowledge-to-policy literature". ODI-IKM Working Paper 5.

3 global.evipnet.org/?page_id=37 (accessed 9 July 2012)

collaborative and asynchronous work spaces. In this context, in 2011, a research group from the Health Policy and Research Unit of the Pontificia Universidad Catolica de Chile, proposed to explore and evaluate the use of Ning, an online platform for creating custom social networks, as part of an alternative and complementary approach to EVIPNet's traditional face-to-face collaboration. Thus the EVIPNet-Americas Online Collaborative Spacewas established to support the process of preparing policy briefs by multiple actors by contributing to the development and creation of work groups, by providing information related to the development of the briefs, and by facilitating the exchange of information among the groups.

The goal was not to produce important changes in the process, but to explore the capacity of the technology to enhance the collaborative work of researchers and decision makers. The researchers from the Pontificia Universidad Catolica de Chile used surveys and interviews to investigate how participation in a custom-made social network influenced the work of EVIPNet.

In the end the tool was used less than expected due to a number of limitations and barriers of the national teams, the context and the way the tools were introduced. Some of the research team's observations are:

The platform competed with other sites and digital tools and the groups opted for more established and familiar tools, such as email, telephone and meetings.

The platform's use was recommended to the local networks, but its use was not obligatory. Interviewees reported that they would have been more likely to have used it if it had been required. This may be because group members were mostly from public or academic organizations which are highly bureaucratized and hierarchical. In a context of multiple tasks and challenges and facing a lack of time, non-mandatory recommendations (i.e. the use of the platform) are likely to be ignored even if they are easy to use, and potentially beneficial.

The facilitators of the national groups are key agents in the functioning of the groups. If more effort had been put into demonstrating the use of the network to them during implementation, they might have been more effective champions of it.

The sense of community among the national groups studied was weak, brief and ephemeral. The participants felt that the teams do not consolidate as real communities in practice. This may be due to the diverse origins of the members (academia and government) as well as to the fact that the government representatives tend to change frequently. At any rate, many of the difficulties of creating face-to-face communities will be reproduced when attempting to create virtual ones.

> *Implementing a software to support social networks to support the development and consolidation of a Latin American network of decision makers in health policy, EvipNet Americas*, Tomás Pantoja Calderón, Mauricio Soto Duran y Valentina Ubal, Research Unit in Health Policy & Systems (UNIPSS), Pontificia Universidad Católica de Chile

GENERATING MEETING SPACES USING WEB 2.0

The Costadigital project, Building the future of information technology for education through the use of web 2.0: developing the 2010-2020 public agenda, explored web 2.0 tools and platforms to "validate strategies used to generate online meeting spaces" in order to promote joint research between researchers and policy makers to establish guidelines for the use of ICT in education. For this, the various steps of the Delphi method were applied through a number of web 2.0 applications, including online forums, blogs and social networking sites.

The Delphi method has enjoyed widespread use for educational research, and is considered an effective and reliable methodology. The method consists of using a series of questionnaires that proceed one after the other, in such a way that the most common responses from each are used in the next questionnaire. These questionnaires are presented to a group of experts on a particular subject in order to reach a set of consensual views, established through statistical analysis. The project demonstrated that it is possible for web 2.0 applications to emulate the face-to-face presence required by the methodology, with minimal modifications to the procedure.

The exploratory research conducted by the project was successful in terms of participation of the invited panel members and the results obtained were in accordance with those that would have been expected when using the same methodology "off-line".

In addition to the adequacy of the spaces built with web 2.0 applications in terms of meeting the experiment's goals, success seems to also be due to many contextual factors such as: the previous experience and legitimacy of the institution that conducted research (located within the Catholic University, Costadigital is specialised unit conducting research into ICT and education); its robust contacts with representatives of the academic community, the government, and other stakeholders (Costadigital was able to invite experts and decision makers and to count on their commitment to remain active throughout the project); and the significance and topicality of ICT and education issues in the Chilean background (education in general has been a prominent issue in Chile in recent years[4] and ICT and education has been an active field for policy design and implementation).

Building the future of information technology for education through the use of web 2.0: developing the 2010-2020 public agenda. Makarena Alzamora, Costadigital, Pontificia Universidad Católica de Valparaiso, Chile.

---

4 See chapter 2 in this volume

BARRIERS IN COLLABORATION

According to Marcia Rivera, lead researcher of the project Researching and building a Dictionary on Social Policies Using Web 2.0 Tools, the relative inattention to the proper use of key concepts in the research sphere, as well as when formulating and carrying out social policies, limits potential for processes which lead to mutual understanding and collaborative work. In order to overcome this obstacle, the project sought to collaboratively build definitions of a set of usual terms in the social sciences. Complementarily to this particular goal, it also sought to establish an environment for virtual collaboration that brings together researchers, decision makers and other stakeholders.

In the first stage, an academic team selected the terms to work on, and proposed the initial definitions (both individually and collectively). These definitions were then published using a wiki platform, which was accessible through the project's webpage that is hosted through the associate institution (CLAEH). It was also promoted through email and Facebook.

The project extended multiple invitations to participate: to academics (10 postgraduate students, 6 university teachers and researchers and 10 regional experts), decision makers (16 ministers of Social Development and their advising teams) and representatives from NGOs that work in the development field (15 people). Most of the invited persons declared their interest in the project, but they did not ultimately participate in writing the definitions of the proposed terms. The research team found three causes for the limited participation: i) lack of awareness of the virtues of wiki tools for collaborative work; ii) frequent changes affecting the ministerial working teams; iii) high-level academics' contributions inhibit the participation of the other parties; and iv) lack of time to engage in the task.

Investigación y construcción de un Diccionario de Políticas Sociales usando instrumentos de web 2.0 Marcia Rivera, CLAEH, Uruguay

MAKING MOBILITY VISIBLE

The project Mobility and access to public services: Towards better coordination and participation, attempted to show the corresponding authorities the importance of understanding matters of transportation from the perspective of access to public services. To use Carden's words (2009), this project exemplified a situation in which "a new or emerging issue activates research, but not policy-makers [...] who remain averse to the research and its promises"[5].

Traditional approaches to public transport identify access to a service as the ability to arrive at the location where the service is provided. However, the so-called 'Geography of Access' uses a more all-encompassing concept, in which access results when an individual is actually able to accomplish what they aimed to do (for example, to attend class or to obtain medicine) and takes into account the length of the trip, competing demands for time, the time of day the service is offered, and other complicating factors. In this way, "mobility" is the result of the interaction of a given mode of transportation with other services, with the user's other obligations and with aspects of the service that the user attempts to have access to. Through a methodological tool called "travel histories", qualitative and quantitative data is collected through semi-structured interviews, providing information on travel habits and access to a service as the result of the interaction between subjective aspects and objective conditions related both to transportation and to the intended activity/outcome. That interaction determines whether or not one or more intended trips are carried out and whether the service is actually accessed and accessible.

---

5 Carden, Fred. 2009. *Knowlegde to Policy*. Singapore: Sage-IDRC.

Case studies included access to health and special education services for persons with disabilities and access to women's health and middle school education for youth up to 21 years of age, in four municipalities of the metropolitan region of Buenos Aires.

The project's communication strategy aimed to provide a "voice" to communities affected by mobility and access issues so they could describe their situation in their own words. Low-cost video equipment and video production software were used to record and edit interviews and the results were posted on the project's website and on YouTube[6] and shown during meetings with local government officials.

The videos were edited in such a way that the testimonials of the affected persons would reveal, both to themselves and to the authorities, the theoretical perspective of the project while serving as powerful demonstrations of the relationship between transportation and access to public services.

The videos were an effective way of communicating research to officials responsible for transportation and public health policies, demonstrating the actual needs of some segments of the population in those areas. They also provided a means to present policymakers with a new approach emanating from academic research, an approach that could provide better solutions in relation to these needs.

Mobility and access to public services: Towards better coordination and participation Andrea Gutiérrez, Instituto de Geografía, Universidad de Buenos Aires.

---

6 www.youtube.com/user/movurbanaysalud

8. THE IMPACT 2.0 IGUIDE

Karel Novotný

In order to see their research findings reflected in public and institutional policies, researchers must be skilled in networking and in communicating research findings to those who make decisions. A lot depends on personal agility and skills in direct relationship building, but communication technologies can facilitate interaction with policy makers and even building working relationships with them. The emergence of web 2.0 tools has revolutionised personal networking and entertainment but it also brings new opportunities in terms of how researchers can open and develop effective communication channels with other stakeholders, encourage discussion and debate of their work, build their own online and offline reputations, and "package" their research findings to more effectively communicate them with policy makers and the general public.

While contracting many web 2.0 services doesn't require much more than creating an online account, researchers interested in using the tools strategically to support their policy-oriented work face a number of issues. Among them are:

- There are serious privacy implications in using many social networking tools where strict separation of private and work domains is difficult and sometimes even counter-productive;
- Web 2.0 tools can be helpful for reaching communities that are already using them, but for various reasons, many of the people we want to communicate with are not. For example, many companies and organisations —including entire government administrations— block their employees' access to some or all of these tools, making them unreachable to anyone who uses web 2.0 to communicate research findings or other key messages;
- The tools change constantly, established services disappear and new ones appear, and accounts, online identities and work habits can seem in a constant and unmanageable flux – creating a state of internal chaos that can cancel out advances in communication and collaboration with external agencies. The same change can also be expensive - requiring tedious and expensive research and testing, or sudden changes in strategies as services disappear or fall out of favour;
- The advertising-funded model of many web 2.0 services generates a huge amount of noise and can be incompatible with the image a research organisation or a government department would like to project.

The ambitious goal of the *Impact 2.0 iGuide* is to help researchers, policy makers and activists deal with some of the challenges mentioned above, and to guide them through the process of choosing tools and strategically implementing them in their communication strategies. This is done by systematising tools and approaches[1]

1 The *iGuide* recognises both web 2.0 technology —web-based applications that facilitate interactive information sharing and collaboration on the web— and web 2.0 behaviour. For our purposes web 2.0 does not refer only to change in the technology of the internet, but also changes in how the internet is used by individuals and organisations.

and linking them to specific researcher policymaker communication scenarios.

WHO NEEDS THE IGUIDE?

The *iGuide* can help you if are a policy-oriented researcher and you want to do any of the following:

- To identify online communication channels currently used by the policymakers and other stakeholders you are addressing with your research
- To encourage discussion, debate and collaboration based on your research findings
- To better understand the policy context, e.g. to identify and understand the main policy actors, to identify key issues, and to recognise opportunities.
- To find out more about people whom you want to address with your research findings
- To connect with other researchers active in your field
- To draw public attention to your research findings
- To build your reputation online
- To present your findings in an accessible format that works for the public and/or for decisionmakers
- To maintain ongoing online conversations with other researchers or policymakers

The *iGuide* is for all researchers who want to increase the impact of their findings, regardless whether they are independent or form part of established research team. Strong communication strategy and strategic use of web 2.0 tools should be embedded in any research process so you are encouraged to use *iGuide* when developing such long-term strategy, not only when you need to 'push' your final research conclusions.

iGuide is published as a wiki which makes it easy for new contributors to edit and add to it. All researchers are invited to contribute to it based on their experience with using web 2.0 tools for linking research and policy. *iGuide* is published under open Creative Commons license which means that everyone is free to re-use, re-publish, and re-distribute it as they need.

CONTEXT, EVIDENCE AND LINKS

The *iGuide*'s organisation is based on the Context, Evidence and Links (CEL) framework, a tool to understand how evidence contributes to policy and practice. Developed by the Overseas Development Institute within its Research and Policy in Development programme (RAPID),[2] the CEL framework argues that influencing policy requires both a research and a communication strategy and that success first requires understanding:

- The political context you are working in: is there political interest in change? is there room for manoeuvre? how do policy makers perceive the problem?
- The evidence you have, or could get: is there enough of it? is it convincing? is it relevant? is it practically useful? are the concepts familiar or new? does it need re-packaging?
- And the links that exist to bring the evidence to the attention of policy makers: who are the key organisations and individuals? are there existing networks to use? What's the best way to transfer the information: face-to-face or through the media or campaigns?[3]

Once you understand these, the next step is to participate in them – to get to know the policymakers and to identify allies

---

2 www.odi.org.uk/RAPID/

3 www.odi.org.uk/rapid/tools/Toolkits/CEL_Presentation/Presentation.html

and enemies in the political context, to understand the evidence used to support the existing policies and to make sure that your own evidence is credible and your reputation is good, and to establish links to other people, institutions and networks you can work with. Doing this, requires a wide range of skills. ODI lists the following:

- **Storytellers:** Practitioners, bureaucrats and policy-makers often articulate and make sense of complex realities through simple stories. Though sometimes profoundly misleading there is no doubt that narratives are incredibly powerful.

- **Networkers:** Policy-making usually takes place within communities of people who know each other and interact. If you want to influence policymakers, you need to join their networks.

- **Engineers:** There is often a huge gap between what politicians and policy-makers say they are doing and what actually happens on the ground. Researchers need to work not just with the senior level policy-makers, but also with the 'street-level bureaucrats'.

- **Fixers:** Policy making is essentially a political process. Although you don't need to be a Rasputin or Machiavelli, successful policy entrepreneurs need to know how to operate in a political environment - when to make your pitch, to whom and how.[4]

All of this requires a lot of work –interviews, meetings, and observation are key to understanding the context, evidence and links, research findings have to be pakaged and repackaged to communicate them to different audiences, meetings and dialogue are essential for establishing and participating in networks... the *Impact 2.0 iGuide* grew from the premise that the internet and web 2.0 can be effectively and economically

---

4 Ibid

applied to these tasks by identifying web 2.0 tools and strategies that can be used to effectively address the many tasks involved in effectively inserting research into policy discussions.

HOW TO USE THE IGUIDE

A researcher's first task is to get a clarity on their specific communication needs, whether it is promoting their reputation as a researcher online, attracting public attention to their findings or starting a communication loop with like-minded colleagues and/or policymakers. Once done, the users should review the CEL framework before turning to the *iGuide*. The *iGuide*'s first point of entry is via the task or goal that you want to undertake: identify potential allies and opponents, build networks with like-minded stakeholders, package new ideas in familiar narratives... All of these tasks are presented in a clickable cloudlike image and a more conventional table of contents on the *iGuide*'s first page.

Clicking on any of the tasks opens up a next level listing specific tools that may help with the task and in many cases providing a short description of how they can be used. Some strategies are illustrated by case studies provided by those who successfully applied them. Entering through the table of contents will bring you to deeper levels with detailed information and tips on, for example, online seminars or webinars as they are known[5].

To give an example, your organisation has generated a wealth of research evidence and you want to incorporate Web 2.0 into your communication strategy to help you "sell" the evidence to policy makers and/or public; Go to the *Evidence* section in the cloud, chose the key activity on which you want to focus (*Building a convincing case and presenting clear policy options*), and chose the specific strategy that will help you achieve your objectives, for example '*have key findings and policy implications*

5 iguides.comunica.org/index.php/Webinars_-_sharing_your_findings_in_online_seminars

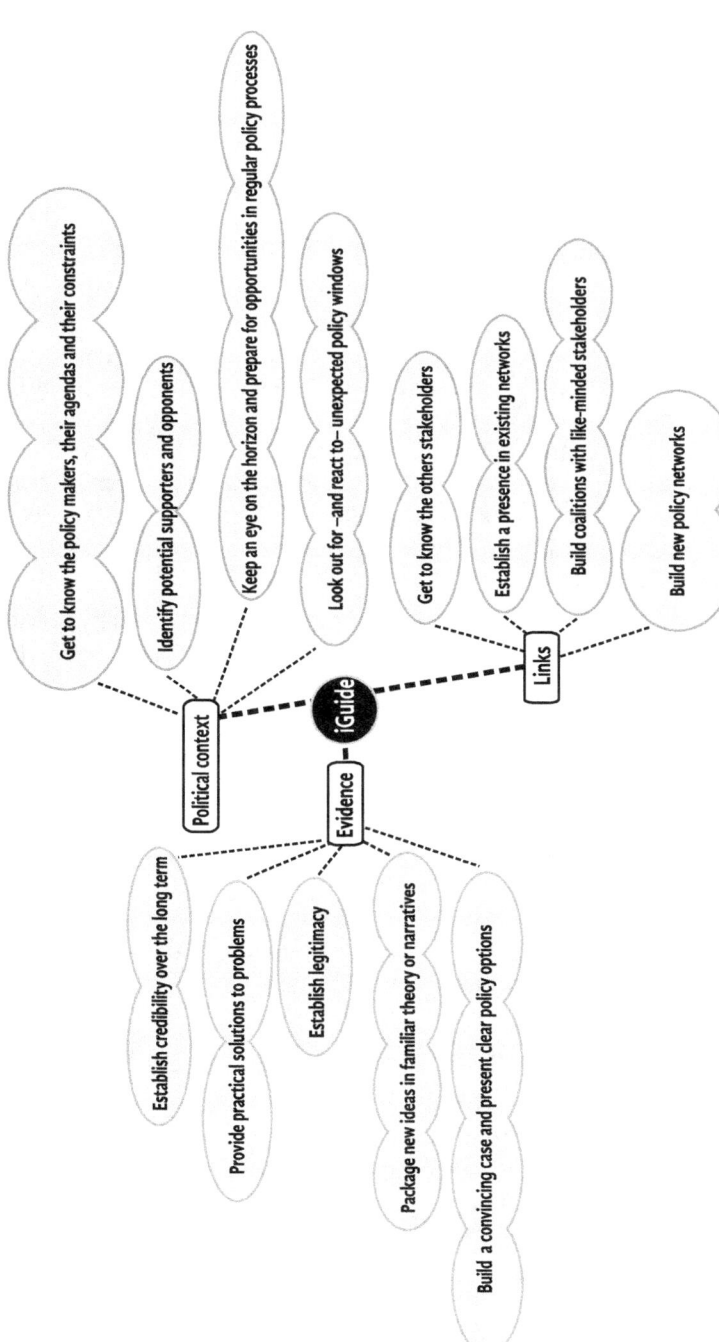

Figure 1: The iGuide cloud lists some of the many tasks you might want to undertake

ready to be presented in a schematic, yet understandable and credible manner'. The section will point you to a selection of visualization tools, online map systems, tools for generating graphs and diagrams and links to online video services where you can publish short interviews about your findings.

Another example is a situation when you need to link with like-minded researchers with whom you wish to collaborate or who will support your cause; Go to the *Links* section, select the key activity on which you want to focus (in this case *'Identify potential supporters and opponents'*) and chose an appropriate strategy - *Identify potential supporters and linking with them, establishing channels of effective information exchange with them and rapidly working on pushing common agenda.* You will be prompted with a list of tool types that will help you pursue these strategies.

If you design your research communication strategy while you are designing your research project itself and make the *iGuide* part of that design from the beginning, you can collect your research data in a format that will make it easy to re-package and present online. The opportunities presented by using web 2.0 tools might also lead you to the decision to include new components in the research process. For example, ongoing publishing about your research progress on a blog or a social networking platform might catch the interest of other key stakeholders (researchers, policymakers), interest them in collaborating with you, and eventually make them more receptive to your findings.

POSSIBLE IMPROVEMENTS AND DEVELOPMENTS

The *iGuide* was intended as a work in progress with the flexibility to change the information about the tools and strategies as new ones emerge. Users are encouraged to contribute to the guide with their own experience, thus helping to maintain it collectively up-to-date. At the same time, the *iGuide* will benefit from additional development that will increase its uptake and impact. Scenarios for possible near future development include:

- Incorporating a section on methodologies of evaluation & monitoring of the impact of web 2.0 tools for reaching researchers' communication objectives. The section will cover also specific tools for impact analysis, as well as tools enabling evaluator to map social networks (e.g. tweetdeck). The same section will include risk analysis methodology that enables researchers to undertake analysis of risks associated with incorporating web 2.0 tools into their research project, and the strategies to deal with these risks.

- Promoting the *iGuide* as a natural hub for publishing case studies and good practices on using web 2.0 tools to link research and policy. Since the use of these tools in given research context is only a very recent phenomena, no online space exists where researchers could review such experience made by others. This plan implies promoting *iGuide* across research networks and finding efficient ways of harvesting researchers' experience. By its design, the *iGuide* lends itself to become THE crossroad linking case studies with information about tools that are protagonist in those cases.

Other plans for the *iGuide* future development include development of blogs and forums where researchers will be able to:

- Share experiences with using web 2.0 tools in policy-oriented research.
- Find help with specific web 2.0 components of their projects, from other researchers.
- Find space to form partnerships and draft new collaborative projects.

Future development of *iGuide* will be guided by real challenges that researchers and policy makers face when implementing web 2.0 tools into their communication strategies. Our experience so far has indicated that the web 2.0 tools are being most efficiently used when researchers/think-tanks use web 2.0 tools to raise public awareness and campaign, as well as to lead public consultations.

Yet another important area of future *iGuide* development is related to new content sections. Authors are planning to include a section on short video production and more detailed guide on using visualization techniques for communicating research findings. Finally, future versions of the *iGuide* will provide practical tips on using web 2.0 tools to develop and manage communities of practice, as well as suggestions for optimum content design and management which increases the impact of using web 2.0 tools in research projects (using the right metadata, formatting, etc).

Impact 2.0 iGuide - New mechanisms for linking research and policy

Original text developed by Cheekay Cinco and Karel Novotný, Association for Progressive Communications (APC). Later versions of the document co-authored by Bruce Girard, Fundación Comunica. Available at iguides.comunica.org

9. ACCESS AND USE OF SOCIAL NETWORKING SERVICES BY PUBLIC SERVANTS IN LATIN AMERICA

Raquel Escobar[1]

THE PROBLEM

When implementing the Impact 2.0 project, we found that many public servants did not have access to web 2.0 tools at work due to restrictive access and use policies in their workplace.

Adoption of interactive and collaborative web 2.0 tools by public administration and government is part of a worldwide process of modernisation of government that began at the end of the twentieth century, with digitized information and the online presence of institutions and government. In this context, the use of web 2.0 tools facilitates the participation of citizens and other outside actors in government activities.

Many of the projects linked to Impact 2.0 worked with publicly available online social network services (Facebook, Twitter, LinkedIn, YouTube, etc.) where sharing content-based materials is relatively simple, as are collaboration and

---

1 Based on research conducted in five countries by Graciela Selaimen (Brazil), Patricia Peña and Marcelo Avilés (Chile), Julio César Mateus and Antonio Capurro (Peru) and María Julia Morales (Uruguay), and on a consolidated report prepared by Alexandra Ayala, Pamela Cruz and Dayana León (CIESPAL).

building network relationships online. They also offer a way of communicating with the general public. When we discovered the restrictions to network access and use of these tools among the public administrations of several Latin American countries, we realized that the issue pointed to several questions regarding the impact of these restrictions. A primary question is how, and how far, these restrictions affect the possibility of using social networks to influence public policy.

Thus, the present study was carried out in five Latin American countries: Brazil, Argentina, Chile, Uruguay, Peru and Ecuador. The study examines policies restricting or permitting access and use of web 2.0 social network services by civil servants in these five countries.

METHODS AND RESEARCH TOOLS USED

Our research combined several methodologies. To start with, five case studies were designed; this qualitative research method allowed an in-depth study of an event, object or case. The case study method looks to explanations of the causal processes involved in the object under study, rather than its effect or the effect's probability of occurrence. For this reason, the main questions in our study focus on why or how the process takes place. We used quantitative and qualitative tools based on possible compatibility and complementarity of these two positions.

The quantitative aspect was covered by surveys which sought to identify use and restriction regulations regarding web 2.0 tools and social network services, either in a specifically selected public entity and/or across the entire public service. The survey was carried out among fifteen public officials at various hierarchical levels within one public entity in each country, regardless of whether they were responsible for managing digital content. There were twenty-two questions in the survey.

The qualitative tool applied was the in-depth interview. Thirty-five interviews were conducted, seven in each country. The questions aimed to establish how the existing policies and regulations on the use and restrictions of web 2.0 in public administration and governance were perceived and why they were perceived that way. The interviews were conducted with key informants.[2]

Based on the surveys, we learned: what rules exist governing the use of online social networks within each office studied, how the interviewees perceive them, whether the rules are written or verbal, and how the tools are used by civil servants.

We also obtained information about how interviewees use of ICTs and social networking tools at work and demographic information such as gender, age, education level, position and responsibilities.

The interviews, with people from government, the private sector, civil society and academia, attempted to uncover information about the possible impact of access rules and perceptions regarding their use in public offices.

PUBLIC ENTITIES STUDIED

In each country the study was carried out within a national or local public sector entity. The entity selection criteria were: that the entity's vision/mission confirmed an ongoing relationship with citizens; the entity's importance in the national context; existing studies on the entity; whether officials were accessible; and whether they were willing to take part in surveys and interviews.

---

2 Interviewees in each country were directors of the selected office and the person in charge of the department of communications or technologies; two people from the academic sector; two representatives of civil society connected to the mission and/or vision of the selected public office; and a person from the private sector.

Bearing the above in mind, the selected entities were:

- Digital Cabinet (Gabinete Digital), Rio Grande do Sul Government, Brazil.
- National Consumer Service (Servicio Nacional del Consumidor) (Sernac), Chile.
- National Assembly (Asamblea Nacional), Ecuador (AN)
- Municipal government (Municipalidad Metropolitana), Lima, Peru (MML)
- Ministry for Social Development (Ministerio de Desarrollo Social) Uruguay, (Mides)

Once the entities were selected, each official website was examined, in order to identify applications used and their function.

The Rio Grande do Sul Government's Digital Cabinet

In Brazil's southernmost state, Rio Grande do Sul, the government's Digital Cabinet project stands out because the participatory tools used allow for cooperation among the governor's office, ministries and citizens.[3]

This is a pioneering initiative in terms of its use of interactive internet tools, both for Brazil and the region. Three components: *The Governor Answers* (questions are sent and the most-voted ones are answered); *The Governor Listens* (citizens hold public meetings and governor listens); and *Collaborative Agenda* (citizens collaborate in drawing up the Governor's and secretariats' agenda by sending in local suggestions and requests).[4]

---

3 The initiative was launched on May 24th 2011, is coordinated directly by Governor Tarso Genro's cabinet at www.gabinetedigital.rs.gov.br, and is "dedicated to promoting direct communication between the Governor and the people."

4 In September 2011, it was awarded the "e-gov" prize for excellence in e-government, in the public e-services category, given by the Brazilian Association of Research Companies.

Also, the Digital Cabinet maintains online social network accounts on Twitter, Facebook and Identi.ca.

National Consumer Service (Sernac)

Sernac is located within Chile's Ministry of the Economy. It seeks to promote and develop a consumer rights-oriented culture. Its current priorities include to improve and modernize its work and to consolidate a consumer protection network.

Sernac's website seeks to improve its institutional communications channels and is part of a constant effort to position its "brand". The website is known and used as a formal channel for providing services to the public.5 It displays Twitter and YouTube links, and users can subscribe to site updates through an RSS service. The main page provides answers to common queries and has a link to the "claims" section where citizens' claims are received and processed. There are several sub-sites such as a *Consumer's Magazine*, a blog, *Sernac Participates* and *Sernac Children*. The official Twitter account is *@sernac*, and there is an email account to receive citizens' queries.

National Assembly of Ecuador

InEcuador the legislative body is known as the National Assembly and has 124 elected members. In accordance with the Transparency and Access to Public Information Act, all National Assembly proceedings are published on its website6, as are the full texts of bills under consideration.

---

5 The website is a source of information for journalists. In 2007, the site had over a million annual visits, a figure that doubled in just two years. In 2009, social network and YouTube accounts were opened. At least 257 videos had been uploaded to YouTube as of 24th September 2011, while the Twitter account registered 91,074 followers.

6 www.asambleanacional.gob.ec

For the Assembly, citizen participation and information transparency are a transversal axis in which ICTs have an important function.[7] Within the framework of a project to develop a multimedia programme, the Assembly has emphasized radio and internet use to comply with a legal requirement to transmit all of its sessions. The National Assembly has added a number of features to their website using YouTube, Twitter, RSS, Facebook and Flickr, all administrated by the communications office that also manage members' blogs.

At present, the site is a principal means of communicating institutional information and in 2008, the portal was awarded the National Union of Journalists' prize in the Communication Technologies category.[8]

Metropolitan Municipality in Lima (MML)

The new municipal government took office in January 2011.[9] The administration began with a clear policy governingweb use, both for interacting with citizens and for ensuring transparency. In February 2010, the Mayor of Lima began using social networks, reaching 4,864 followers on Facebook and 23,928 followers on Twitter. The site was awarded first place in the 2011 report on transparency portals carried out by a citizens' ombudsman measuring levels of compliance among regional and municipal governments throughout the country.

---

7 This policy and web 2.0 use, however, were not born with the Assembly. They were inherited from the Constitutional Assembly (2007-2008) who constructed blogs for Assembly members and members of dialogue panels, broadcast live and promised to construct a sphere for public participation which would be inclusive and representative.

8 The prize was awarded for "work representing the first effort to integrate the resources of an information portal with the new trends in social webs" (ecuadorin-mediato.com 2009).

9 The Metropolitan Municipality of Lima a specia provincial level entity. It includes the capital city, with a population of more than 7.5 million, almost one third of Peru's entire population.

At present, the website,[10] displays an institutional description, information on the city and metropolitan area, and offers guides for administrative procedures. It also provides news and describes municipal projects and programmes.

To enable online activities, it links with service portals belonging to various entities and administrations in the municipality. It also offer ombudsman services and access to municipal data. The website also links to the municipal presence on YouTube, Facebook and Twitter.

Ministry for Social Development (Mides)

Ministry for Social Development (Mides) was created in 2005 by Law N° 17,866, which defines it as the entity "responsible for national social policies, and the coordination, both on sectoral and territorial level, of coordination, monitoring, supervision and evaluation of plans, programmes and projects, within its competence, promoting the consolidation of a progressive, redistributive social policy."[11] At present, Mides uses social networks (Facebook, Twitter), RSS, an institutional websiteand YouTube. Some programmes also have their own Facebook and Twitter accounts.

Germán Barcelona, head of the Department of Information and Communication states that: "At Mides, we are attempting to migrate to e-governance, a target shared by the ministry and the entire government. There are two aspects involved: on the one hand, designing our web portals (...), and on the other, the social networks which open the way for interacting with citizens. This is our challenge".

---

10 www.munlima.gob.pe

11 www.mides.gub.uy

OVERVIEW OF RESEARCH RESULTS IN THE COUNTRIES STUDIED

As was explained in the introduction, this study explores the ways in which the policies of restricted access and use of social network services in public entities in Latin America may impact coordination and action dynamics when designing public policies.

We will therefore begin with the problem's contextual variables, in order to establish the scenario and conditions within which the impact mentioned above is observed. Analysis of the variables is carried out on the basis of the research findings.

Young people behind the screens in public entities

The surveyed population was mainly young: 60% are between 25 and 30 years of age. Following Sinclair and Cerboni's evolutionary scheme establishing the relationship between user age and ICT, these people would belong mainly to "digital native" and "digital adaptive" generations[12].

Forty-three per cent of the surveyed population is responsible for managing and/or organizing contents and/or communications channels on social networks or other applications. Most (80%) of those who produce content are between 25 and 35 years of age.

In this sense, then, the outlook is favourable for the use of ICTs in public entities, particularly when considering that a considerable number of managerial positions (7) are held by digital natives or adaptives.

---

12 The digital adaptives generation is that of people born between 1965 and 1979, when PCs and video games appeared; they are now between 32 and 46 years old. The digital natives generation (born between 1980 and 2000) use technologies perfectly well and are between 11 and 31 years of age. The digital immigrants generation is born between 1946 and 1964 and is between 47 and 65). Finally the digital avatars were born this century. (Taken from "Ciberactivismo de movimientos políticos y sociales en Ecuador. Informe de estudio", Quito: CIESPAL, Sept. 2010, p. 80. See also www.saladeprensa.org/art998.htm).

Features of the access and use policies for social networks services

This variable has several features: the presence or absence of restrictive policies; whether they are written or verbal regulations; the focus of existing, identified policies; their reach; and the qualifications of the people subject to them.

In the surveys applied to public servants from the five public entities studied, 56% (42 of 75) said that there were internal regulations or rules referring to the use of, and access to, online social networks.

Regarding the characteristics of these policies, we are can affirm the following:

- There is strong commitment to an institutional policy tending to protect the entity's "brand" and to ensure that internet use does not negatively affect productivity.

- Access and use policies are generally expressed verbally, rather than in writing.

- Policies regarding access and use often respond to the vision or perspective of the person in charge of ICT within the entity at a given moment, that is to say, they can be arbitrary and are not established by formal policy.

In this situation, which we shall describe in depth below, 48% of public servants are favourable towards the regulations in their offices, qualifying them as good or very good.[13]

---

13 Only in Ecuador is there a majority saying they are "very good"; in Brazil and Chile, the majority feel they are "good." Only Brazil and Chile report people who say they are "bad"; and in Peru, those not replying to this question are over half (8) of the surveyed population.

Greater productivity, less participation?

Several different criteria explain the situation of web 2.0 and social network access and use. In Chile's Sernac, optimizing computer use and "brand" protection were the reasons given to restrict access to the internet and social networks. At Peru's MML, on the other hand, productivity alone is mentioned as the reason for restricting access.

All of the people surveyed in Ecuador's National Assembly have access to the internet. Nevertheless, there are also objections to this widespread access as it is thought that internet availability may lead to lower productivity as staff might use social networks for personal rather than legislative purposes.

Optimization and productivity criteria are present in the answers given by public servants in three of the five public entities surveyed. Interestingly, public servants tend to hold a favourable opinion regarding these performance-oriented restrictions.

Are online social networks used to inform, or for interaction?

With the exception of the Rio Grande do Sul's "Digital Cabinet", use of social networks is primarily to provide information and not to interact with the public.

For Chile's Sernac, the website is a key ally in carrying out the institutional mission, and is used as a formal channel for providing services to the public and information to journalists and the media.

For Ecuador's National Assembly, the internet is "an alternative means of communication and a tool for transparency and a public accountability" and this is reflected in its website and its institutional accounts on Facebook, Twitter and Flickr.

For Peru's MML, the portal and web applications provide information and guidance for Lima citizens.

For Uruguay's Mides, the internet is a channel for information about the various programs and activities they implement.

The overall approach is information-oriented, and this has led to underuse of social network services, simultaneously strengthening unidirectional links between the public entity and citizens. This is clearly seen in Sernac, for example, which closed its institutional Facebook account because consumer claims were overwhelming available resources, and only use its Twitter account to receive messages or complaints. Websites and social network accounts at the MML and the AL have become an alternative way for authorities to communicate their agendas and for the publication of official documents. This is a rather uninspiring scenario in terms of interactivity.

On the other hand, although the Rio Grande do Sul's Digital Cabinet also uses social networks for informational purposes, their project was constructed as a digital forum for direct and two-way communication with the Governor. Its purpose is to "articulate a digital culture," for which it uses different dynamics and possibilities. For example, the platform brings together three social network services (Facebook, Twitter and Identi. ca) to enable public comment on specific subjects, to bring the Governor closer to the public and to hold public hearings based on questions asked on or off-line. In this public entity, however, staff did mention limited technical access in that insufficient computer resources are available for their use.

Between unwritten rules and formal regulations

With the exception of Sernac, where they have instructions to keep to a "single discourse" online, and the Mides, where they have a protocol to unify the style for presentation and drafting of news published on the web, the public entities studied do not appear to have any express rules on content to be posted to social networks. This may be due to the fact that working with web applications is a relatively new matter.

Other guidelines found are: in Ecuador, for the use of blogs as "backbones" to sustain other web applications; in Uruguay, for creating other digital forums to allow for faster and more direct access to services; and in Peru, for preventing use not related to work.

Surprisingly, no mention is made in these guidelines of the time to be spent connecting and interacting with citizens on social networks; although most of the officials we surveyed reported they spend less than one hour per day interacting with citizens online.

Another series of guidelines identified in the institutions is related to specifically banned content as well as technical limitations, such as limited bandwidth, security for wireless access and a scarcity of computers in the institution.

Referring to this, both the sample survey population of public officials and those interviewed consider that the use of social networking services promotes citizen-government interaction, in that it allows for the exchange of requests and proposals seeking to resolve collective needs. However, in the case of Chile, the deputy director of Sernac's office states that neither interaction nor collaboration are government objectives: "We have to be faithful to our legal mandate and provide public services, which we do through the appropriate channels."

SOCIAL NETWORKS IN MULTI-SECTORAL COORDINATION DYNAMICS FOR POLICY DESIGN

This section will look at the mechanisms through which social actors might participate in the development of public policy using online internet social networks.

We will also be looking at the perceptions of social actors (private sector, civil society organizations and academia) on the way government institutions use social networks in aspects connected with openness and responsiveness.

We also attempt to establish whether social network restrictions and use rules are based on an institutional plan with a focus on promoting interaction, or only on providing the public with information. That is, we attempt to see whether the policies might lead to the construction of participatory procedures through online technologies, or only adapt institutional procedures to technology.

ICT policy, institutional dynamics and collaborative technology

Although the majority of those surveyed stated that they were aware of the various ICT tools, it is clear that the same is not true when referring to access. In every country, the number of public servants with access to social networks at work is much lower than the number who are familiar with the tools.

In Sernac in Chile, for example, staff are not allowed to use any social networks and very few content services. Professional networks such as LinkedIn and communication services such as Skype are also blocked. Only 9% of survey respondents in Chile stated that they use email.

Out of the total number of public servants surveyed in the five entities studied, 68% reported they had email access, far less than the 93% of those who said they were familiar with email. This is due to policies restricting access and, to a lesser extent, to limited availability of equipment and technology. Brazil provides the only case where all respondents reported using email.

Of the social networks used by the institutions for contact with citizens, Facebook and Twitter are most commonly used, respectively 39% and 35% of respodents reported using them at work.

Brazil and Ecuador are the countries where use of Facebook (13/15 and 8/15) and Twitter (13/15 and 8/15) are highest, as they are for blog use (8/15 and 6/15). Other services used at work by those surveyed are Skype and RSS feeds, with 15 people using each (20% of the population surveyed).

The Rio Grande do Sul Government's Digital Cabinet is the entity where more people have access to all tools, followed by the National Assembly in Ecuador. Access at the Sernac in Chile is low: only 7 of the 15 surveyed use email, not one uses social networks and very few visit blogs or use YouTube.

External views on how to create an environment for coordination and participation through internet use

In the interviews carried out with members of the private sector and with civil society and academic organizations, ideas were expressed in relation to establishing principles, rules and regulations to define the access and use of web 2.0 tools in public administration:

- To create feedback mechanisms for citizens and interactive forums;
- To foster interaction with users through online forums and talks;
- To find a balance between access, connectivity and training for all social actors who are members of participative and democratic governments;
- To take into consideration the experience citizens have acquired regarding social participation through internet and social networks, and using it.

Responded also mentioned was the need for training, stating that training is needed not only so public servants learn how to use the tools, but also so they learn to value their potential for interaction and collaboration and connecting public administration with citizens.

CONCLUSIONS

Faced with the fact that internet access and social network services use are restricted for public officials working in administration entities in Latin America, the research we presented has attempted to answer the following questions:

- How much, and how, do these restrictions influence the management of public policies?

- What evidence accounts for this influence?

- Have any possibilities for interaction among the different social actors and public entities been created through participatory exercises for managing public policies by using web 2.0 channels?

- Restricted social network use among public servants is connected to a narrow vision of the possible uses of these tools, among other reasons. Indeed, their use has been largely limited to transmitting and disseminating information, and reproducing unidirectional communication modes.

- Informal guidelines provided by managers influence how, and what for, public servants use social networks. This influence is more powerful than formal policies governing the ICTs by the public administration in each country. Features of these guidelines include:

- Intense commitment to an institutional policy tending to protect the entity's "brand" and productivity.

- The use of social networks in public administration falls

under a predominantly one-way informational framework.

- Regulations on access and use rarely appear in writing; they are usually verbal.
- Frequently, these policies respond to the personal vision or position of the managers in the entity regarding social networks, rather than being established public service policies.
- None of the entities in our survey allows internet and social network access for all its civil servants.

Civil society's perception of the use of social networks by public entities is that there is only limited potential because of public administration resistance. Civil society actors stressed the need for demonstrating the interaction and collaboration potential of the tools for connecting the public administration and citizens.

The civil society actors we consulted in the survey consider that it is necessary for public officials to undergo training, and that this should be accompanied by practices that would seek to promote mechanisms for citizen communication and interaction, to go beyond the simple transmission of information.

Finally, in this context, one of the factors limiting the use of social networks to dissemination may soon be challenged by demographics. Most of the public servants participating in the survey, and some directors, belong to a generation of digital natives or digital adaptives and as they move into positions of higher management, this could translate into better knowledge and understanding of social networking in public entities. And eventually into a more innovative use of online social networking services.

THE AUTHORS

Eduardo Alonso has a masters degree in political science from the University of the Republic in Uruguay. He is a researcher with the project "Uruguay 2010. Telecommunications: between access and innovation" of the Program for Communication Research (PRODIC) and "Fundamentals of Partisan Democracy in Uruguay" of the Political Science Department, both within the University of the Republic. As a researcher, consultant and speaker he specialises in communication policy and new technologies and on the relationship between republicanism and political parties in democratic theory.

Eduardo Araya is associate professor at the University of Valparaíso in Chile. He is currently completing a PhD from the Open University of Cataluña. He has a Masters in Political Science and Public Administration from the University of Chile. He has taught undergraduate and post-graduate courses in the principal universities of Chile. Recent research and publishing work is centred on the use of ICTs in Chilean politics, and the reform of the state, the civil service and oversite institutions.

Estela Acosta y Lara studied inguistics at the University of the Republic in Uruguay. She has edited and translated numerous academic works. She has experience in computational linguistics, discourse analysis and science, technology and society.

Diego Barría is completing a PhD at the Institute of History of the University of Leiden in the Netherlands. He has a Masters in History from the Catholic University of Chile and of Public Administration from the University of Chile. He has taught at the University of Chile and the Central University of Chile. He has published widely on administrative reform, both from a historical and current perspective, social participation in policy formulation processes in Latin America and on the use of the internet in Chilean politics and administration.

Federico Beltramelli has a Masters in Political Science from the University of the Republic of Uruguay and is a PhD candidate at the Faculty of Journalism and Communication at the National University of La Plata (Argentina). He is associate professor, coordinator of the audio-visual area of the undergraduate Communications Programme of the University of the Republic and researcher with the Program for Communication Research (PRODIC).

Jorge Bossio has a Masters in Business Administration (ESAN) and in Political Science with a Specialisation in International Relations from the Catholic University of Peru (PUCP). He has broad experience in information and communication technologies and communication for development. He was a member of Peru's telecommunication regulator (OSIPTEL), of the National Committeee for the Information Society, of the regional top level domain administrator (ccTLD), and other national and international committees related to the internet. He has been the coordinator of DIRSI (Regional Dialogue on the Information Society), a researcher with the Institute for Peruvian Studies and with the Catholic University of Peru, where he also teaches. He is currently editor of the La Mula internet portal.

Raquel Escobar has a degree in Communication for Development from the Simon Bolivar Andean University of Ecuador and another in communication and informational society Simon Bolivar Andean University of Bolivia. She is currently Director of Sustainability and Planning of the International Centre for Superior Studies in Communication for Latin America (CIESPAL). She teaches courses in communication and research planning at the Central University of Ecuador and communication and health at the Catholic University of Ecuador.

Bruce Girard is founding director of Fundación Comunica. He has published widely on various aspects of communication, communication rights, and participatory communication. Among his books are *A Passion for Radio*, *Global Media Governance* (with Seán O Siochrú and Amy Mahan, 2002), *The One to Watch: Radio ICTs and interactivity, and Communicating in the Information Society*. Girard studied communication at Carleton University and Simon Fraser University (Canada) and was resident researcher at Delft University of Technology (The Netherlands). He is a member ex-oficio of the Executive Council of the International Association for Media and Communication Research (IAMCR) and a consultant to international agencies including UNESCO, UNDP and FAO.

Karel Novotný is a Knowledge Sharing Projects Coordinator of The Association for Progressive Communications' Strategic Technologies and Network Development Programme (APC-STaND). He is leading or is involved in number of projects related to Web2.0, community (low-cost) access to ICTs, online security and privacy, and others. Karel is sociologist and lives between Montevideo, Uruguay and Prague, Czech Republic.

Fabro Steibel PhD in Communication Studies by the University of Leeds (UK), under the supervision of Prof Stephen Coleman, Fabro Steibel's research interests focuses on digital citizenship and media policy regulation. He is currently the Director of Communication Studies at the Universo University, in Rio de Janeiro. He was a visiting researcher in the UCSD Department of Communication, under the supervision of Prof Daniel Hallin (2009), and he has previously worked for research projects on media policy and communication studies funded by the European Parliament, the UK Office of the European Commission, the Oxford Reuters Institute for the Study of Journalism, the UK Royal Trust, the Brazilian Government (Capes) and the EU Fundamental Rights Agency. His main publications include a report and two book chapters on the UK 2010 Leaders debate (authored with Prof Stephen Coleman and Prof Jay Blumler), and a book single authored published in Brazil on regulation of political advertising in the country.